Someone You Love Is Dying

Someone You Love
Is Dying

A Guide for Helping and Coping

by Martin Shepard

Harmony Books

a division of Crown Publishers, Inc.

New York

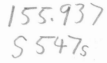

155.937
S 547s

ACKNOWLEDGEMENTS

Publisher: Bruce Harris
Editor: Linda Sunshine
Production: Gene Conner, Murray Schwartz

Harmony Books, a division of Crown Publishers, Inc.
419 Park Avenue South
New York, New York 10016

Copyright © 1975 by Martin Shepard
Printed in the United States of America
Published simultaneously in Canada by General
Publishing Company Limited

Library of Congress Cataloging in Publication Data
Shepard, Martin, 1934-
    Someone you love is dying.

Bibliography: p.
    1. Death—Psychology. I. Title.
BF789.D4S48   155.9'37   75-22088
ISBN 0-517-52375-2
Third Printing

Mac Shepard was an illustrator who died at home on May 14, 1972, after a prolonged cancerous illness.

Many of the sketches that accompany this text were made during his final hospitalization.

Martin Shepard
May, 1975

Other books by Martin Shepard:

> *The Love Treatment*
> *A Psychiatrist's Head*
> *The Do-It-Yourself Psychotherapy Book*
> *Fritz*
> *Beyond Sex Therapy*

and, with Marjorie Lee:

> *Games Analysts Play*
> *Marathon 16*
> *Sexual Marathon*

From my father
Through my sons

The quotations that appear throughout the text have been culled from many sources including books, films and personal conversations. Some of the quotations are from famous sources, others from relatively unknown ones, for we have used any which we felt offered valuable insights.

Contents

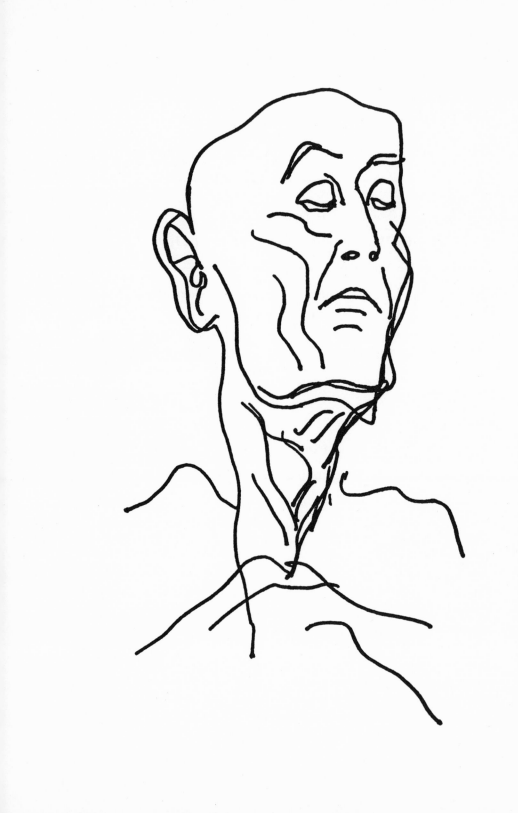

1

Someone You Love Is Dying

The act of dying is also one of the acts of life.
—Marcus Aurelius

I LIVE NEAR a bay in eastern Long Island in an area populated by farmers, beachcombers, and a host of wild animals. One sees hundreds of rabbits each year, but never any dead ones. Pheasants walk among the rye grass and potato fields. Occasionally one of them is struck by a passing car. "Poor bird," I momentarily grieve, and pass on, aware only that all other pheasants I've encountered are always quite vital and alive. One summer, the body of a swan lay in the field across the street. I assumed it broke its neck on a high-tension wire and died unnaturally, for whoever sees a dead bird unless a bizarre accident has occurred?

Like humans, the other beasts that inhabit this world have a habit of dying privately, beyond the sight of passersby. It has been calculated that each square mile of temperate sky contains twenty-five million insects that fly and float in a great column of air. They die relatively quickly. Some are buried in the bellies of their fellow creatures; others disintegrate and fall to earth, but it all takes place without our noticing.

Most of us start off at a disadvantage because we regard death as a calamity. When we, our relatives, or our friends are confronted with a fatal illness, we view it as a serious affront; some unnatural act or divine unfairness that, with better luck, precautions, or more competent medical care might have been prevented. For all of our being a part of a vast, expiring horde of humanity, where sixty million people die each year, we are reluctant to abandon the concept of death as some strange and avoidable catastrophe. We search for causes instead of accepting mortality as part of the cycle of life.

Now, someone you love is dying, and you're not quite sure how to react. You want to be helpful, but you're uncertain as to what helpfulness consists of. You yourself feel a jumble of emotions. Despondency, helplessness, anxiety, resentfulness, guilt, and aversion are natural. So is the feeling of being overwhelmed.

You must wonder, of course, how the dying person feels, and yet you are reluctant to ask. You probably try to emit a basic optimism whether it is felt or not. Have you shared your own apprehensions? Or do you avoid the subject entirely?

What you feel and what you do depends upon the ill person as much as upon you. It is important to understand his or her thoughts and feelings as well as your own. You are to an extent like dancing partners, exerting subtle influences upon each other, guiding at times and following a lead on other occasions. The dying one and you can exchange real feelings, play act, support, encourage, or burden each other, depending upon your individual temperaments and awarenesses. Coping with your emotions is intimately related to coping with the other person's, for like mirrors, we tend to reflect each other.

How we ultimately respond is dependent not only upon past history but also upon how we typically deal with both adversity and the unfamiliar. We bemoan our misfortune, are fearful, grow angry, shed tears, or use the occasion as a growing experience. Those who have witnessed death before—who have been close to a dying relative or friend and have shared experiences of what it was like—are in a better position to act constructively, for familiarity dispels many dreadful fantasies. With firsthand knowledge you learn that the reactions of the dying are less harrowing than you might have imagined. Dying people make good teachers, if we allow them to talk to us. They not only help us to judge death as a natural process but let us know what comforts and what distresses them in their last months, weeks, or hours.

My background includes medical school, a general internship, and fourteen years of psychiatric training and practice. During that time I've had ample opportunity to physically attend the dying and, later on, to hear tales told by the bereaved. None of these experiences, though, were as helpful as living out my father's dying with him. By our open sharing of reactions and concerns I soon realized that he was the authority on death, not I. Freed from the need to play "expert," I became an appreciative student. Among the things he taught me were that death was neither as painful nor as terrifying as I had been led to believe.

It is not easy to have such intimate contact with death. People may not wish to die out of sight, yet most of them do. Studies have shown that the great majority of dying humans wish to die at home, in familiar circumstances, surrounded by family and friends. Yet we typically shunt off our relatives to nursing homes and hospitals where they expire without us. The Center for Death Education Research at the University of Minnesota recently surveyed 560 hospital deaths and discovered that in most instances no family members were present at the bedside; that survivors generally learned about the passing through the phone call of some nurse or clerk. This traditional isolation is not only the dying person's loss but ours as well, for we are deprived of an opportunity to learn some fundamental lessons.

It is this lack of familiarity with the subject of death, and a fear of unknown elements, that contributes in large measure to our feelings of dread and indignity when death impinges upon us. The greater our familiarity, the less our terror. The less our terror, the greater the likelihood that we can provide comfort to friends and family who face death, and the greater the probability that we can survive their passing with minimal distress on our own part.

To overcome our fears we must also understand those factors that reinforce them. The child has to contend with stories of bogeymen who haunt the night. The adult is subjected to constant reminders of violent endings on films, television, and in the newspapers. Religion tells us that we will suffer the tortures of hell for our sins upon earth. Freud and Marx, who both dismiss belief in an afterlife as nothing more than myth, undermine whatever comfort we might gain through thoughts of immortality.

> The crash of the whole solar and stellar systems could only kill you once.
> —Thomas Carlyle

Someone You Love Is Dying is an attempt at reappraisal. It proposes to give practical information regarding the everyday details involved in preparing for death, ways of minimizing fear, grief, and the difficulties of the post-mortem period. It provides a forum in which people can share their firsthand experiences so that the unfamiliar need no longer hold such dread. It is also a book that encourages alternatives to the traditional ways in which we treat our dying, by focusing upon

alternate dialogues, treatments, and locales in which dying itself may occur.

The circumstances of death, today, are too frequently anonymous and ignominious. Death ought to be the punctuation
point of life, not some obscure footnote. If we are to help
make "death with dignity" a reality rather than a slogan, let
us begin to listen to those who have faced it. They are the
ones who are likely to tell us how it's done.

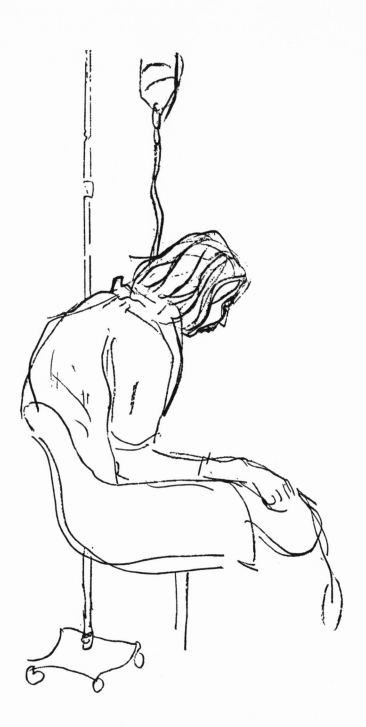

2

Why Me?
Why Anyone?

(Facing Death at 25)

"WHY?"

This question reverberates endlessly in the minds of all concerned when death is imminent.

Why must it happen in my family?

Why must it happen now?

Why must it happen at all?

And just as *you* ask "Why?" you may be sure that the fatally diagnosed is likely to ask the same question.

Hubert is a dark-haired, slim, freckled-faced, twenty-five-year-old law student of medium height and clean-cut good looks.

He had a malignant melanoma removed from his back a week before our meeting in his hospital room. A chain smoker, the tips of his thumb and index finger on the right hand are stained with nicotine.

In a clipped, precise, detached tone, he presents himself as a good attorney might. His brief is prepared and he touches all bases. It is hardly necessary to ask him any questions at all. He has, like a proper counsellor, prepared himself to accept any ultimate Judgment.

*   *   *

Hubert: Last summer on the beach I was with some friends of mine and this girl pointed to something on my back which was freckled in a pattern; in a ring. She said, "What's that on your back?" And I said, "Aw, I've had that for years."

"It looks like cancer."

"Come on. I've had it for years," I answered, and I never gave it another thought. Some two months later, into the fall, I developed this itchy rash and it sent me to the doctor. While I was there he noticed the ring. I said, "Oh, by the way, what is that?," recalling what the girl had said. And he answered, "It's something called a pigmented nevus. If it remains the same, we leave it alone. If it doesn't, we do something about it."

He treated my rash, which went away. The ring of freckles did not, and I monitored it. I felt it. In the beginning you couldn't distinguish it from the surrounding skin. I read in the *Encyclopedia Britannica* about skin cancers. One of the things it said was that it has different characteristics from the surrounding skin and it felt different. So I figured as long as it felt the same, it was all right. However, one day it began to feel different. Two black spots appeared. It was originally composed of a ring of brown things. Two of the brown things suddenly weren't brown anymore. They were black.

And then it began to develop thickness. I felt it, day by day. Bumps were developing. These two black things were growing up. So I called up my own doctor, the one who had spotted it, and I said, "Listen. I want you to send me to someone for this pigmented mole on my back." He remembered right away what I was talking about. He never said "Why?" I suggested a surgeon. He said, "No. Try a dermatologist first," and he gave me the name of one. This was only a month ago; a remarkably short time.

I'm trying to think of what I was thinking between then and when I went in to the dermatologist. I know I wasn't happy. I read about melanoma in the 1960 encyclopedia. It didn't say much. Just how you could seldom detect them. And it said, "Although they are easily accessible, survival rates seldom exceed 25 percent." I never thought of myself as a particularly lucky fellow, and I never thought that I was going to be in the lucky 25 percent.

Then the day came for my appointment with the dermatologist. I very much hoped he would do what a surgeon did when I went to him eight months ago with a lump in my neck, which was to feel it and say, "I'm not impressed by it. It's nothing." I not only hoped but thought he might do that. But he didn't. This dermatologist did the medical equivalent of hitting the ceiling. He said, "It's got to be cut out. Right away!"

I asked, "Well, don't you want to take a piece? Do a biopsy? Make a test?" And he said, "No no no no. Don't touch it. We need a big piece. Go to a general surgeon. Who's your regular doctor? I'm calling him up!" He really threw a scare into me. And then he threw in a sentence, "It could be a type of cancer." He didn't have to tell me that. I knew what it could be and what type.

Well, at that point I figured I was really in for it. I went into a depression, although apparently nobody noticed it. I figured my number was really up. I began to get a lot of very fanciful, romantic thoughts. I thought of all the poets who died early: Keats and Shelley and Byron. I thought of their work. I've never believed in a hereafter, and I didn't start to. I thought of ways in which I could make myself immortal. If I could write something that would be left behind that other people would remember, I wouldn't die completely. I also had an experience of seeing myself differently, physically. I always had a secret vanity, but now I saw myself as almost pitiable.

I remember being in the criminal courthouse in Baltimore, which is a busy place—cops, defendants, lawyers hanging about —filled with smoke. It always gave me a good feeling, and it's got a lot of glass in it. I saw my reflection and I thought, "There he is. A nice young fellow. Dark hair. He used to walk around the courts. Gee. Isn't it a shame. What a pity he died." You see, I don't like self-pity. So I saw myself as someone else and felt sorry for him.

Marty: You were kind of detaching yourself. How did you feel inside, though? Was there more than depression? Did you cry? Were you scared? Were you very anxious?

Hubert: I was sad and somewhat anxious. I almost quit smoking, but I sure threw that out the window. I remember a scene from a western movie of a guy who was going to be hanged that day. For his last meal he was having too much strawberry ice cream. His co-defendant said, "Yur havin' too much. But yur going t'be dead before you kin be sick." I figured, "What the hell. Cigarettes aren't going to get me. I'll be dead before that anyway."

I didn't cry. I didn't tell too many people, because I had this idea of dying in the middle of life and I didn't want a string of mourners around. I didn't tell my girlfriend. My roomie I did tell because he saw I was acting strangely, and ventured, "Something must be bothering you." And I was glad to tell him. I told my parents the following day, after I went to see the surgeon.

That surgeon pulled no punches. He said, "It will require aggressive treatment. Surgical removal might not be enough. We might have to do a very wide excision and cut out a lot of skin. Or we may have to take out some lymph nodes." I

asked very calmly, "Oh? Are there any nodes in the area?," for
the thing was in the middle of my back. "No," he answered,
"from the groin." And I guess this had been building up in
me, for I began to faint. He yelled for the nurse, who came
into the examining room. They put me on the table, the nurse
took out an ammonia snapper and put it under my nose, and
I was all right. The first thing I said was "Forgive me. I hate
bad news." He said that he would get me a hospital appointment, and then I went back to work.

That further increased the assurance that I wasn't going to
make it. Then I began to fear not death, but a slow, painful,
lingering death, and I began to consider taking my own life.
If I learned for sure from a competent medical authority that
I was going to go, I didn't want to do it that way.

I entered the hospital eight days ago. They began to do tests
right away, which started to come in negative. The very next
day after that they scheduled the biopsy. They didn't wait. I
developed a kind of fatalism, I guess. I ceased to worry. I
figured I was here. It was out of my hands.

Then the tumor man came down. There were other people
in the room. I sent them out. I wanted to be very straight with
him. I asked, "What about it?" "Well," he said, "there's a good
chance that you'll walk out of here cured. And there's a chance
that you won't. We'll do everything that we can for you." He
was very reassuring. The fact that he was young, that he looked
me in the eye . . . you know, the fact that nobody was keeping
anything from me. He also said I was entitled to my fears.
Hearing that from everyone was also nice. I didn't have to
put up a bluff front.

The biopsy was done under local anesthesia. They shot me
full of Demerol, which makes you not give a damn about anything. They could have said, "All right. Turn him over and
cut off his nose." I wouldn't have done anything. And the
surgeon said, "You're doing very well. Everything's going fine."
As he's working I feel him, but it's like a very remote pressure
through a thick blanket. That was in the morning.

I'm lying around and I sleep the rest of the day because of the Demerol, and the small incision doesn't hurt. Then I get a phone call. It's from my mother. She said the biopsy results were very encouraging; that the surgeon had told her that. She asked the surgeon, "May I rejoice?" and the surgeon said "Yes." And I . . . I don't know . . . I felt good, but I didn't feel that good. I didn't let out a whoop, or anything like that. It was almost like I also expected that I would be all right. The next morning, the surgeon himself came in and gave me a scientific analysis of what I had, using terms which I understood from all the reading that I had done. "What you have is entirely isolated," he said. "It rarely metastasizes. It's just the most innocuous type, and you're very lucky."

Marty: So at this point you're not worried about having a fatal illness?

Hubert: I wouldn't say it's 100 percent clear. There are times when I find myself waiting for the other shoe to drop. I keep asking for confirmation. I got strong confirmation from the doctor, who said, "To the very limits of medical knowledge, you don't have it anywhere."

I really feel I've been brought back from the brink. And I'm glad. But I'm not going to do anything different. I'm really not.

Marty: Before this happened, at any point in your life, had you thought about death much?

Hubert: I thought about it as unimaginable. It's impossible to imagine being dead.

Marty: So you didn't walk around with any fear of it? Wondering if you'd ever make it to twenty-nine or thirty?

Hubert: Sometimes I would get morbid fears like that. I'd sometimes wonder, "Am I cut out to make it all the way? Am

I one of those people whose life line is short, only they can't see it?" But I figured there sure wasn't any sense worrying about it.

If you're twenty-five and you know for sure it's going to happen, well . . . I would comfort myself with thoughts that I had done just about everything I had really wanted to do. I feel I'm better off than those poor guys who died in 'Nam at eighteen or nineteen. I had a few more years than they. Sure, I'm being cheated out of years that other people have, but maybe they don't enjoy those years anyhow. Maybe I'm better off now. You know the old motto? Live fast, die young, and be a pretty corpse.

Marty: Is that what you'd tell people who have to come to terms with death prematurely?

Hubert: Yeah. I heard that young people—young women who discover a lump in their breast—always say "Why me?" Kurt Vonnegut wrote a book called *Slaughterhouse Five,* about American prisoners in Germany. He has a scene in which they are being marched into a barracks, and out of nowhere one of the German guards smashes one of the Americans across the face with a rifle butt. The American picks himself up out of the snow and says "Why me?" And the German answers, "Vhy you? Vhy anybody?" Well, why anybody? It's got to be somebody. Melanomas happen. Maybe they're floating around somewhere and they just stick onto people. Why you? Why not the next guy? 'Cause to the guy in front of you, you're the next guy.

Marty: Did you tolerate the initial news better than you thought you could?

Hubert: There was no one moment; the news came in bits and pieces.

There was one low point, when I left the dermatologist's office. That was really deep, deep depression. But I didn't stay depressed that long. Maybe till the end of that day. And I would force myself not to dwell on it. Yet it would come up from time to time. I often would find myself thinking of very material things. Of girls. And I would think, "What am I thinking about this for? I should be thinking about profounder things: Eternity. God. Why was I thinking about that girl's legs?" But I was. Life went on. And my vital powers hadn't left me in any way at all.

*   *   *

> As soon as a man comes to life,
> he is immediately old enough to die.
> from *Der Ackerman aus Böhmen*

"Why must this come to pass?" Because, as Hubert aptly put it, "It's got to."

Witnessing a child, an adolescent, or a young adult die can be a particularly painful process. "They are being taken prematurely," we are likely to think. "They've not yet expressed their full potential."

Yet often the young who face death find it easier to accept than their survivors do. And why shouldn't they? Is a flower that blooms for a day any less full and beautiful than one that lasts longer?

Life is a moment between two voids. How one lives their alloted time helps determine how that individual approaches death. Though only twenty-five, Hubert has led a full life, for he has done most of what he wished to do during the years he has had. And that richness of living has provided him its own support.

"Why should I be healthy and someone else seriously ill?" is another thought that frequently arises. Implied in this question is an unarticulated element of blame and guilt over surviving. "It's my fault," one is likely to feel. Or it's the fault of a parent, spouse, child, or physician.

Such soul-searchings are natural and understandable occur-
rences. They haunt our minds for a while but eventually pass.
"Why not my life instead?" Because it's not your time yet. Nor
are you selfish for staying on this earth a bit longer.

The notion of any individual going on indefinitely, no
matter how much we may wish it, is both an absurdity and
an impossibility. No circumscribed entity that we know of in
the universe lasts forever. Stars and galaxies form and dissolve
within their lifetimes just as we do. Their span, though measured in billions of years, is, given their enormous size, not
necessarily longer than the life of the mayfly, which lasts for
one day, or the lives and half-lives of subatomic particles, some
of which measure in billionths of a second. Life must be
measured by how well it fulfills its potential, be it as a tree, the
sun, a man, woman, or some winged insect; not by the arbi-
trary standard of measured time that humans have invented.
And life is also measured by the way in which we die.

3

What Do You Tell
A Dying Person?

THE QUESTION OF whether or not to tell people that they have a fatal illness arises frequently. Much has been written on this subject and many statistical studies have been done. These clearly indicate that standard medical practice and common social assumptions are out of phase with the wishes of the dying. This disharmony can create additional stress during the preterminal stages of illness.

J. M. Hinton, in an article in the *Journal of Psychosomatic Research* (1966) entitled "Facing Death," cited one study at a tumor clinic where 560 patients were asked whether they would wish to know of a fatal diagnosis. Eighty percent desired this information, 12 percent didn't, and the remaining 8 percent were unresponsive or uncertain. Another sampling came from a Minnesota survey of one hundred cancer patients and one hundred noncancer patients. Eighty-nine percent of the cancer patients wanted to be informed if they had inoperable malignancies, and 82 percent of the noncancer patients wished to know if they ever developed a fatal tumor.

Among doctors the opposite occurred. Eighty-eight percent of 219 physicians polled at Chicago's Michael Reese Hospital had a policy of not giving out a patient's grave prognosis. In a similar sampling of 444 Philadelphia physicians, 12 percent never gave out a diagnosis of cancer, 57 percent usually didn't, 28 percent usually did, and only 3 percent always proffered the truth to those they saw.

The reasons these physicians gave for withholding this information were that sharing the news of impending death would create "too much stress," or that "the patient couldn't handle it." It is, in fact, clearly the doctor who can't handle it, who cannot look his patient in the eye and acknowledge his impotence to stave off the illness.

My medical training led me to view death as an avoidable disaster, as some enemy which, given a proper course of treatment, might be overcome. To acknowledge that the battle is a losing one is not easy. Nor is this admission any easier for family members, many of whom also harbor irrational feelings of responsibility and failure when death is imminent.

Further reluctance to share a terminal outlook stems from vague hopes that somehow this troublesome fact will disappear. Like the frightened ostrich that buries its head in the sand, we pretend that subjects unlooked at will vanish.

Several excellent studies have shown, however, that the overwhelming majority of informed patients adapt favorably to news of their illnesses and that the uninformed are not only usually aware of the nature of their disease but often learn of it from outsiders. The price paid by those who are not told is greater. They frequently suffer the distress of uncertainty and find themselves unable to share their fears with others. As one of the dying I interviewed put it, "I firmly believe that the only thing worse than knowing you have cancer is thinking you have it and nobody telling you one way or the other. That is enough to drive you right up the wall." The uninformed may not have sufficient time to make final arrangements and bid special farewells. They are also deprived of choosing the locale in which to spend their final weeks.

Lucille was a woman in her late thirties who died one year ago. Some two and a half years before, she was hospitalized and treated for symptoms of anemia, weight loss, and weakness. Her doctors and family conspired to keep the true diagnosis from her because it was an illness she had always been quite fearful of. They told her instead that she was run down, and medicated her, with only partial success. She continued her usual activities, as best she was able, for the next year. She also kept a diary.

The following entry occurred several months before her death. It not only emphasizes the potential cruelty of deception, but also underscores another of the reasons why many avoid the subject; that the loss of someone else threatens our own sense of security. We see, too, that regardless of a victim's fear of sickness, such fears can be overcome when candor is provided.

Slowly my life began to take shape again. What I had so easily dismissed before became important once more. My family and friends gave me the impetus to regain my strength and become involved with the business of living.

The horrible struggle began. I battled with a mind eager to live against a body that refused to cooperate. Suddenly their opposite directions became one. My spirit surrendered completely to my physical disaster.

I was in my room sorting the day's mail. Letters of

lesser interest were casually tossed aside as I read others first. Then I opened one I initially dismissed and glanced at it. It was a medical insurance form filled with the standard required information. I started to fold it to return it to its envelope when one word on the other side glared at me.

Its power strangled me; I was paralyzed in its grasp. I was transfixed by each letter burning into me. Over and over I turned the page, hoping to find some unseen separation that would detach my name on the front from the disease on the back. The diagnosis was leukemia.

The word fragmented my entire being as if I had been struck by an exploding bullet. I screamed.

My mother-in-law and my housekeeper came rushing into my room. I held myself to try to touch and ease the pain so deep within me. I screamed again. "Not this way. Not this way. Let me die now . . . quickly!"

The world was no longer mine. It could not touch me, and I would not reach out for it. I withdrew completely.

Fear possessed me. Crying, I awakened every night for weeks and weeks. I prayed for death; I bargained for death. Death became my constant companion. I offered my hand to death to lead me away.

The human spirit betrayed me. The will to live would not be corrupted. It would not allow me to turn my back on life. Where was I to go? My life before had vanished. My body was no longer familiar. My future was stifled.

What human being has the right to force another to live on false premises? How can the dignity of truth be denied to anyone? However harsh it may be, it is more cruel to live a lie.

The most difficult task was the struggle with the acceptance of mortality . . . indeed, mine. But, although

I know why my life will end, we *all* do not know when. This awareness makes the end of the road less formidable, and it serves to make what lies along the way more meaningful. Those around me who cannot be at peace with their own, and inescapable fate, are more uncomfortable with me than I am with myself.

Clearly, one must balance candor with kindness. If someone has undergone a prolonged diagnostic procedure or exploratory surgery and never asks what was found, that person probably belongs to the 10-20 percent bracket that choose to avoid knowing their final fate. But anyone who asks a direct question ought to be given a full and adequate answer. If honesty and integrity are valued in living, should they be defiled in dying? When relatives, friends, or doctors presume that they know what's best to tell a dying person, they disrespect the moribund individual's intelligence, character, and courage. They also shut the door on meaningful communication that might lessen the loneliness of dying.

Telling someone the truth alleviates tension among the living as well as the dying. "I was so relieved to finally ask Al how he felt," recalled the brother-in-law of a fatally ill man I spoke with. "For months I didn't know what to say when I was around him. Did he know or didn't he? We had always been quite close, and now there was this great formality and strain between us.

"When my sister told me that he knew, I ran over to their house. We had a good cry together. I told him how much I worried about him. And it's been nice ever since between us. I don't have to go about watching every word or expression I make lest I let the cat out of the bag."

Integrating the awareness of death and the living out of remaining time is not the easiest of tasks. It is ultimately an individual trip, for no companion may join the dying person. The traveler typically traverses landscapes fraught with emotional turmoil before finding ultimate peace and acceptance.

The job of the living is to follow them as far down the road as is humanly possible.

When my father first became ill, the doctors felt it was appendicitis. They took him to surgery and discovered, instead, that he had a perforated carcinoma of the colon. He remained in the operating room for several hours while a sizable portion of his large intestine was removed. On returning to his hospital bed he opened his eyes and asked me, "What was it?"

"Cancer," I answered.

"Thanks." He smiled weakly and dozed back off again.

Some members of my family were upset with me for my timing, for telling him the facts so abruptly. But is there ever a good time for conveying this news? For me the Zen adage that "The kindest cut is the swiftest one" makes eminent sense.

Those relatives who presumed that my timing was off more likely put themselves in his place. We all tend to judge another's inner reactions by our own. This, however, denies individual differences. Instead of presuming to know my father's response, I made my commitment to honesty. He asked and I answered. It was as simple as that. Later on, he expressed appreciation for my trustworthiness; for his being able to count on me for truthful information throughout the course of his illness.

One cancer specialist I know, when asked by patients what they have, invariably responds, "a tumor." Those who wish to go no further, who prefer to deny their possible demise or wish to pause before getting a fuller report, are usually satisfied with that answer and pursue the matter no further. Most patients, though, will then ask, "Is it malignant? Is it cancer?" At that point he will give an honest yes, along with supplying answers and details to all questions asked.

Forthrightness is feared because no one likes to be the bearer of grim news. Yet a lack of candor when questions are directly asked contains more pitfalls than does straightforwardness. Even the 20 percent who initially don't want to know about a fatal disease come to recognize that they have one.

Dr. Elisabeth Kübler-Ross, a thanatologist who has worked with over nine hundred dying patients, reports that only 1 percent continue to deny their diseases to the end. Indeed, most people, as the final hours approach, have been able to forecast exactly when they are going to die.

What greater frustration can there be than receiving get well cards when you know that you never will, than wanting to share your final feelings, only to be met by a smiling someone who says "Don't talk like that. Don't be morbid. You'll be better in no time?"

What do you tell a dying person? The truth. Only honesty will establish trust and open channels for real communication, communication that can be so free of game playing that it often becomes the most intense and intimate form of exchange that people will have in their lifetimes. This potential for intimacy ought not to be denied those who are leaving life. The truth, after all, won't kill them. Their illnesses will.

Who should do the telling? Whoever is asked. When should you do the telling? Whenever you are asked. How should you do the telling? With as much sensitivity as you can muster and in as direct a form as possible.

4

I Never Lost My Sense of Humor

(An Older Man's Story)

I have never wanted to see anybody die, but there are
a few obituary notices I have read with pleasure.
—Clarence Darrow

UNDERSTANDING THAT ONE has a fatal illness is not necessarily
as calamitous as we might fear. For all the difficulties of adjustment, both initially and along the way, telling someone
the truth invariably helps them to gain the perspective necessary to face death, to get it together philosophically.

"People get born and they have to be prepared to die someday," as Jack, a man with a medically incurable malignancy
points out in the following interview. That does not mean
that people invariably dwell on their ultimate passing or that
they enter a perpetual state of depression. Just as no one in

35

good health would continuously think of their final moments, neither do those who are ill. No human being could tolerate facing the fact of ultimate death constantly, nor is it avoidance when he chooses to direct his vision elsewhere.

> If the rich could hire other people to die for them, the poor could make a wonderful living.
>
> —Yiddish proverb

In talking to dying people, I was constantly reminded by them that life does indeed go on. And I was repeatedly made aware of their capacity for laughter, particularly at their own expense. This is something we should not deny them. Candor is not inconsistent with moments of comedy. A belly laugh or two is as good a release from tension as are tears.

> Death is nature's way of telling you to slow down.
>
> —Madison Avenue definition

Four years after my dad's operation, he was readmitted to the hospital because of obstruction of the common bile duct. The obstruction was caused by slow progression of the original malignancy, and caused a blockage of the gall bladder. During one of my visits I asked if I could feel his belly; feel the massive gall bladder that grew bigger daily.

"Sure," he said, lying down and pulling up his pajama top. "I'll show you where they've been poking," he added, forgetting that I was a doctor.

I put my hand on his abdomen as he breathed out forcefully, pushing the swollen, obstructed organ beneath my fingers. I looked down at his belly. The jaundice, deeper with each passing day, had colored his skin a deep yellow. He would obviously need new surgery.

"Well," I said, "at the very least, you can always get a job working in a Chinese restaurant."

We both laughed heartily.

A few months before he died I was told a secret by a member of my family. When I visited my dad that evening I related the story to him, prefacing it with the words "I was asked not to tell this to anybody."

"Don't worry," he answered, breaking out into a belly laugh. "I'll carry the secret to my grave."

> Dying is the last thing I ever expect to do.
>
> —Fred A. Pankrac

Jack is a lumbering, sixty-five-year-old contractor, about five-feet eight-inches tall, with balding gray hair which he combs forward toward his eyes. He too is consoled by his humor, his perspective, his commitment simply to go on with daily living, and by the same hope that never seems to leave any of the dying I've spoken with .

*   *   *

Jack: I have multiple myeloma, a bone disease. Prognosis is from six months to one and a half years. Maybe now it's a little longer, up to three years sometimes.

Marty: When was this diagnosed?

Jack: About six months ago. I had a fall and I forgot about it. Then I got some aches in my back. Not in the usual place where you get backaches. This was up a little higher. I thought that was due to the fall, so I went to my family doctor and had an X ray taken which did not show anything. Two weeks later

I went to an internist who took X rays and blood tests and told me my blood was producing too much protein and I should be further tested in the hospital. At that time I knew that if you produced too much protein, the horrible disease is cancer, which everybody is afraid of. And I realized—it just came on me—that I had it. I went to the library and got a few books out on cancer while I was waiting to get into the hospital. A few days later I was admitted and had the books with me.

Within half an hour, after taking a spinal with the best hematologist in the city, I was told that the diagnosis was multiple myeloma, cancer of the bone marrow, and these cells were making holes in my spine.

We have three daughters, who suggested to the doctor that I was not to be told, that they would break it to me easy. But I understood. As soon as the internist told me that I was manufacturing too much protein, I understood.

So when the doctor came into my room after having a pow-wow with my daughters and my wife, I told him "Look. You tell me. I can face it. You tell me the truth. I want to have it straight so that I can arrange my affairs." So he told me, "You have multiple myeloma. It is a disease of the spine and we have a treatment for it. Sixty percent will take the treatment, 40 percent do not." He built it up. "We have cases as long as seven years . . ." et cetera, et cetera. He left the room and I looked it up in one book, which said six months would be my best bet. And, well, I didn't take it too well.

Marty: How did you take it? What did you think? How did you feel?

Jack: I think I was in a very fortunate position because of my general lifetime philosophy. I was able to rationalize that life is part of death and death is part of life, and if people get born, they have to be prepared to die one day. And I said, "Well, if you have a good healthy life, you will not be afraid of death." I had a good healthy life. I was never sick a day in my life, never had any serious diseases. I had a healthy attitude toward

life. I always enjoyed life and I thought, "It's not so terrible.
Everybody dies."

I stayed six days in the hospital and that was my attitude. I
had a good cry, naturally, when I found out I had myeloma,
but then I just braced myself and said "That's it." And I
haven't been afraid.

Marty: When you had a good cry, what were you thinking of?

Jack: I was just thinking it was too bad that I had to leave here
so soon. I would have liked a few more years, but if I have to,
I have to. Then I said to myself, "Look. You know the chances
of your conception were a billion to one." And then I went
through life when many times I could have died.

I was not born in the United States. In the First World War
my little town was a battleground. We saw soldiers in the
prime of life getting killed. I saw death all around me during
my formative years, so I naturally was braced for death. In fact,
I remember a time when the Russians left and the Germans
came into my village. I was about ten years old at the time.
My father was in the United States and my mother, my three
brothers, and I lived with my grandparents. When the Russians
were leaving, my mother and grandparents were afraid they
would take it out on us; they raped and often killed Jews.

My grandmother never read *War and Peace,* about the Russians' scorched-earth policy. So when she got worried in the
middle of the night, she hid my mother and older brother in
one place and hid my younger brother and me—he must have
been about five—in the barn and locked the front door from
the outside. Her reasoning was that if they see a locked barn
there is nobody there, so they would leave us alone.

I remember watching through the boards and seeing two
Russian soldiers stop with torches in their hands. One took
the house across the road and one went to the barn. We were
elevated slightly and it must have been after a rain, for he
tried to get up but could not and slipped down. He tried again
and slid again. He finally took some benzine and threw it on

the ground and then threw the torch at the barn. The other fellow said, "Come on. I got my job done. Let's go before we are too late and the Germans catch us." They left. The torch burnt out, but the fire never started.

So there was one chance I could have died. I was lucky to have another sixty years of life, close to sixty. And throughout life, how many times are we close to death or near accidents? So I was lucky.

But also, you think of how to save yourself, even though the experts say you are going to die. There may be alternate treatments for cancer. I looked into them and I am trying some of them.

Marty: Which ones are these?

Jack: One is a diet of natural raw fruits and vegetables. The theory behind it is that there are certain things in food that the human being needs. It may be enzymes or other factors that we don't know, and we just boil them away. As soon as I got out of the hospital I got volumes and volumes of books on cancer research. I finally came across this diet and got hold of some medical doctors who do believe in it. Then I got myself interested in Wilhelm Reich, the psychiatrist, who did something with cancer in the forties. He made sense to me with his orgone theory. And it gives me hope because I am trying. I am trying both of them and I feel very well now. I am in good health. In fact, the last time I saw my doctor he said the medicine was working. I usually go every six weeks and take chemotherapy. They give me steroids.

Anyway, something is working. I feel well. There was a time I could not lace my shoes. I could not bend over. I was always in pain. Now the pain has left me. In fact, I even went back to doing some work.

There are hundreds of alternate treatments to cancer besides the orthodox medical ones. Perhaps they do people good because they are positive. They say you will be cured and how

about the people who do get cured? Perhaps someday people
will find out that the mind can cure if you do some positive
thinking.

Marty: So you had a lot of pain, but it's left you since you
started taking chemotherapy.

Jack: It could be my diet. It could be the chemotherapy. It
could be the orgone therapy. It could be my sister-in-law who
sent a fifty-dollar bill to a rabbi in Jerusalem to pray at the
Wailing Wall for me. Who knows? This scientist background
we all have insists we don't know unless it's proven.

I cannot prove anything. I don't know if I am cured. Once
in a while, in cancer cases, one out of ten thousand, somehow,
miraculously is cured.

There are forces in the universe I don't understand, and
some may make sense in terms of cure.

Marty: Do you find that people treat you differently?

Jack: Oh yes. I found, to my dislike, that people show up very
sympathetic, very nice, and sort of pity me. I could never take
that. My friends, my very good friends and relatives, were sincerely frightened. They just don't like to see a situation of this
sort, and they really felt bad. So as soon as my doctor told me
that I was doing fine, that "if the medicine keeps doing for
you what it is doing for you, you may have seven to ten years—
who knows?", I came home that day and decided I would call
all my friends. I was on the phone all day long and I said,
"Look. My sickness has been arrested and I am very, very
happy and I am sure you would like to know about it." Now
they all treat me as normal, which is just what I want.

I will give you an example. My cousin and I are very close.
When she came to the hospital to see me, she took it so bad
that she left the room and started to cry. I knew that, so I put
my gown on and followed her. It seems she just could not

take it. She felt as if it was a funeral. I said, "Look. I got a few more months. Wait for the funeral." I even joked about it. I had a good laugh.

I joke about my illness. Some very good friends of ours went away for the weekend with us when I first decided to go on the diet. Friday night we were in a restaurant. I said, "It's very nice that friends come together to help a fellow at the beginning of a diet." So I took my orange juice and said, "Let's drink!" Selma, sitting next to me, said, "Don't forget, Jack. You invite me to the end of your diet." I looked at her and said, "Selma. I will feel very bad if you don't come to my funeral. I am inviting you right now." And I laughed.

An hour later I realized that what was comedy to me may not be a laughing matter to her.

Marty: A certain sense of humor helps you get by.

Jack: Yes. I never lost my sense of humor. I remember one time when so many people were calling me up and I asked, "Now who told you I had cancer?" "Oh, your brother did." I told my brother nicely—he visited every day—"Look. You're not getting rid of me so fast. So don't tell anybody. Suppose I fool you and don't die. Won't you feel bad about it? So don't advertise it. People may feel bad."

I still enjoy life. I know I am going to die. I don't know when. But somehow, back in my mind, I also think I am going to lick this. Maybe I can urinate on my doctor's grave.

Marty: You said you wanted to know from the doctor so that you could make plans. What plans have you made?

Jack: If I felt I had three months to live, I would like to know what to do with my house. I always wanted to go and see certain things before I died.

Marty: Are you planning these things now?

Jack: No. I am not planning, because I'm feeling better and I don't think I am going to die so fast.

Marty: So your life has basically not changed.

Jack: No, because I enjoy doing what I have been doing. Like going away for the weekend with good friends. We go to the theatre. We go folk dancing. That is part of life and part of enjoying life.

Marty: And if you had any advice for people, would that also be to go on doing what they have been doing?

Jack: I say do what you have been doing all along, even though you think you have not enjoyed it. Get up in the morning, make breakfast. Be with people. Be with your wife. Be with your children. That is life. No high-in-the-sky living. There is no such thing. I never believed in a utopia.

Happiness to me is everyday living: seeing and loving your family, doing what you like to do, learning something.

*   *   *

> Everything comes to him who waits—
> among other things, death.
>   —Francis Herbert Bradley

Aside from sharing an ability to joke, Jack makes several other points that bear brief comment, like the matter of solicitous reactions. "I found, to my dislike, that people show up very sympathetic, very nice, and sort of pity me. I could never take that." His not welcoming this extra attention and concern is a common response, though hardly universal. Another might value such reactions kindly.

Men, more frequently than women, feel uncomfortable when placed in a position of passivity; where because of incapacities or circumstances others inquire about or have to perform small tasks for them. This not only emphasizes their infirmity but also threatens a self that has overvalued concepts such as independence and strength. "I am the one born to be your comforter and sustainer," such a personality decrees, "not the reverse."

Pity has had a tough time of it lately. Considered by some to be a base and deprecating emotion, it is summarily dismissed with a resentfully reflexive "I don't want any." Yet what is wrong with feeling sorrow for another's misfortune? If there are elements of "there but for the grace of God go I" in it, what of it?

We all instinctively grieve for ourselves and others through one another. If Jack's cousin cries while visiting him, does it matter so much whom she cries for and in what proportions? And when Jack follows her out into the hall to comfort her in her distress, are his feelings and motivations any different from hers? I think not.

Of even greater import is the way Jack's story underscores the importance of truthfulness.

To begin with, he enabled his physician to be honest by his insistence, when talking to him, that "You tell me the truth. I want to have it straight so I can arrange my affairs." Without those remarks it is likely that Jack would have been misled, particularly since his daughters requested that he not be told. Doctors traditionally give false reassurance because of their own anxieties and their not realizing that most dying patients would have it otherwise. It becomes, then, most important that someone make it easier for the treating physician to be candid.

Being forewarned makes it possible for Jack to contemplate his unfinished business, to begin to plan for the sale of his house so that his wife needn't, and for preparing to "see certain things" before he dies. Knowing he can do this provides him with true reassurance.

Jack is also free to attempt alternate treatments, such as his diet and orgone therapy. This contributes to a feeling of affecting his own longevity, of coping effectively by leaving no stone unturned in his attempt to survive a bit longer. Whether such measures are physically effective or not is, for the moment, immaterial. Clearly, they are psychologically helpful, for they contribute to an optimism in the face of finality.

We are accustomed to "either-or" concepts. Something is either black or white or gray. Linear logic insists that our thinking either be consistent or we are denying something. Yet modern physics teaches us that seemingly illogical opposites may also be true, as when light is best understood by describing it in terms of continuous waves *and* discreet particles.

One can thus know the truth and still be optimistic. Nor is this "pathological" or "escapist" thinking, for the mind can entertain many thoughts at once. As Jack puts it, "I know I am going to die, but I also think I am going to lick this."

> We are but tenants and . . . shortly, the great Landlord will give us notice that our lease has expired.
> —Joseph Jefferson

> If you are small, death may quite likely overlook you.
> —Somerset Maugham (at eighty-four)

EPITAPHS

Here lies John McDonald.
Born a man,
Died a grocer.

—On tombstone in Scotland

*

Stranger, regard this spot with gravity.
Dentist Green's filling his last cavity.

—Anonymous

*

Here lies a poor woman who was always tired.
She lived in a house where help wasn't hired.
Her last words on earth were "Dear friends, I am going
To where there's no cooking, or washing, or sewing.
For everything there is exact to my wishes,
For where they don't eat there's no washing of dishes.
I'll be where loud anthems will always be ringing,
But having no voice I'll be quit of the singing.
Don't mourn me now, don't mourn me ever,
I am going to do nothing for ever and ever."

—Anonymous

*

Here lies my wife, a sad slattern and shrew;
If I said I regretted her, I should lie too.

—On tombstone in a Yorskshire Cemetery

*

5

Experimenting with Miracle Cures

(Where There's Life . . .)

. . . THERE'S HOPE. AND there is still the process of living. Since in one sense there are no dying people, but only living ones, we need to appreciate how the awareness of death affects the present-day lives of those we care about.

A premature retirement from life is not only demoralizing for the ill and their potential survivors but is also unrealistic. Although survival rates for various diseases can be tabulated on charts, no individual is a statistic. Again and again, chronic killers such as cancer, advanced cardiovascular disease, and biochemical disorders like the collagen diseases fail to fell their

victims according to schedule. One may be at the point of
death and stage a remarkable comeback. People can and have
lived for two, three, four times or more the months or years
estimated for them. And, rare as they are, spontaneous remissions have occurred in all these illnesses.

> It is more important that we live than
> that we die. In fact, dying is of no im-
> portance whatsoever, since it is so tem-
> porary a condition.
>
> —Samuel Johnson

The doctor who tells you that your relative has six months
left may help you confront an impending demise, but his pre-
diction is by no means certain. Death might occur in six
minutes or six years. How the remaining time is spent is often
more important than how long that time lasts.

> Neither the sun nor death can be
> looked at with a steady eye.
>
> —La Rochefoucauld

A constant focus on death is painful, for it is life denying.
It is as unrealistic and damaging as denying that time is running out. We can receive comfort, then, in knowing that nearly
everyone who has been given the news of incurable illness
manages to put it to some creative use. That includes the
survivors as well.

For example, neither the sufferer nor those who care for
them get as bogged down by the trivialities of life. There is
often not only a greater intensity of relationships but also a
much finer appreciation of things that are normally taken for
granted. One becomes grateful for walking, for an appetite, for
children at play, for simple kindnesses, for being able to man-

age elementary toilet functions. We often marvel at the seemingly inconsequential only when these capacities are jeopardized.

> I've often thought that people should go through a cancer ward once a month to be aware of their trivialities, complaints, and their putting people down.
> —Lynn Caine

A consciousness of death can also creatively cut us free of timorous restrictions. When either the ill or the well recognize life as a transient state, they become reluctant to postpone things for a tomorrow that might never arrive. They don't wait for a more convenient time to resolve differences with parents, to tell friends that they love them, to take children on the outings they've promised and never delivered. Instead they fully savor life's experiences. Knowing that this particular show will last for just so long, they begin to make the moments count.

> Expect an early death—it will keep you busier.
> —Martin H. Fischer

One man with leukemia I talked with managed to discover who he was and to be that person only through receiving his diagnosis. A creature of habit and programing, as most of us are, he had lost touch with personal values in his search for a security that life never offers.

"I suddenly asked myself what I was doing," he said. "Why was I working at something I didn't enjoy? Accepting abuse from a boss I didn't care for? Building up a bank account that would do me no good in an afterlife? Hiding my thoughts from other people? Pretending to be one way when I felt another?

"Feeling I had little left to lose, I started to declare myself. I'd say 'No' to things I didn't care for, and I began to pursue those things that truly interested me. And life has been a ball ever since.

"I don't know how much longer I have, but whatever time is left is lived with a freedom I never imagined possible. And I see how I was a prisoner of my own fears before. When I started being my own person, the world didn't fall apart at all. I'm working now at something I really enjoy, and my wife and truest friends have shared my joy as I've evolved."

There is, finally, the searching for alternatives that some doomed people and their families engage in. This is not to say that all these searches are creative. Many are not. There will always be misguided saviors and opportunistic fakers about who make a living out of the grief of others.

The science of cryonics, for example, looks toward a future when bodies, preserved by freezing at the time of death, can be thawed and cured by new medical discoveries. The cost? In 1971, the Cryonics Society of New York charged $8,500 for initial preparation and storage of a body with a thousand-dollar-a-year maintenance fee. Although this may comfort the dying rich, it seems particularly ill suited for anyone else. Even if the terminal illness were eventually treatable, freezing invariably occurs too late to prevent the irreparable brain damage that follows within minutes of heart failure. Tens of thousands of dollars seems a lot to spend when the most one might hope for is a thawed vegetable.

Nonetheless, alternatives to medical treatment that are not particularly costly make a certain sense to me. Once a physician acknowledges that he has no cure for an illness, by what powers does he insist that no one else ought to treat it? If I have learned one thing in the course of my medical training, it is a certain humility in the face of what we doctors do not know. There is often a "party line" on acceptable treatment. What the American Medical Association describes as quackery one day might be considered valid the next. Acupuncture is one recent example. Furthermore, experimenting with the "impossible" is what progress is all about.

Al, one of those doomed experimenters, is a forty-six-year-old six-footer with thinning white hair. He looks like an ex-football linebacker. He suffers from a rare form of connective-tissue cancer that is inoperable and invariably fatal. His wife, Marge, is a plucky and straightforward woman half his size, not quite five-feet tall and weighing less than one hundred pounds. They make an odd, but obviously loving, couple. The interview occurred in their home.

* * *

Al: Eight months ago I experienced being at the point of death. But as time went on, my life span seems to be extending as my health is getting better. I seem to have forgotten a lot of the hangups that I had now that I've gone through it. It's only been three or four weeks that the pains have almost left me.

Marty: How close to death were you? What was your illness?

Al: My doctors and family both felt I was very close to it. It began about a year ago. I thought it was from overwork. At the same time I was dieting and losing weight. I had no other thing to think about in terms of being sick, because I was never sick a day in my life. I just kept losing weight. Then I felt something was wrong with me internally. I had an examination with my doctor, and he confirmed the fact. He couldn't take care of me in his office so he sent me to the hospital for some tests. About the third day in the hospital he diagnosed cancer—or a tumor growth—in my stomach area, and said I had to be operated on immediately.

When they opened me up, because of the location, it was inoperable. It's called a retroperitoneal sarcoma. So they closed me back up and hoped for the best. At that time the doctor told my wife that there was nothing they could do. They thought radiation treatments would help, but evidently [they] didn't help at all.

I got very little sleep under radiation treatment. I was always in pain. I would wake up every two or three hours and take Darvon for pain. People in that clinic would sometimes refuse their treatments. There were thirty-four treatments in all, five days a week.

As I was going through and finishing radiation and knowing that it didn't help, my wife heard of some doctor in Texas who has performed some good in restraining tumors or making them disappear through a different type of therapy, through taking root herbs internally. It's called the Hoxie treatment. At that time we both felt I had nothing to lose.

Now a step like this is taken by a person in desperation. It's not recognized by the medical societies. I could just about walk to the airport. We just about made it. Just standing up caused unbearable pains in my whole body.

Marty: What happened in Texas? Did it help you right away, or did it take a while?

Al: No, it did not help me right away. I still had that feeling that my time on earth wouldn't be too long. When I went down I spoke to this doctor and explained my condition. He gave me examinations and said, "Well, I've heard of it, but it's not that unusual."

We tried to get information from him about his successes with this type of treatment. He didn't try to impress us in any way. He just laid the facts on the table. I asked him, "What are my chances?" and he answered, "I hope to treat that tumor and shrink it. Those are my intentions." As far as longevity is concerned, he didn't give me any deadline.

Marty: Was it very expensive?

Marge: No. It was $585, including six months of medicine. He could have asked for any amount of money and we would have paid it.

Marty: Did he tell you to stop the other treatment?

Marge: No, no. As a matter of fact, he said. "You can go back and tell your doctor. It's your business. I'll correspond with him. I don't know your doctor; you know him better. Some doctors get very hurt and very touchy about this sort of thing. You have to deal with your man yourself and do whatever you like." He said to call in three months. And when I called and told him that the doctors here were very, very amazed . . .

Marty: Did this man tell you his tonics would work right away?

Marge: No. He said to expect relief in three months.

Marty: And how long did it take?

Marge: Three months. When I told him the tumor is not growing and that our doctor said it's getting smaller, he said, "Then don't bother to come down. But come down definitely again in six months." That's in two months.

Al: The pain went on for three more months. One night I woke up at six o'clock in the morning and I couldn't believe it. I actually slept the whole night without pain. I was amazed. I thought, "I've got to have pain." And I felt my leg and my body, and *no pain!* This was part of my recuperation.

Marge: Anyway, with the herbal medicines and the chemotherapy, he's doing very well. So naturally we feel very hopeful. But even as I feel hopeful, every day I think, "When is it going to reverse?"

But who knows what works? Everybody believes in something else. Who is to say what helps? One day we went to a baseball game and met a young woman who was a Jehovah's Witness. She had a sick child who she felt was helped by their healing process: the adults fast for three days and a bunch of children offer a group prayer. She saw Al looking so emaciated that day he practically had to be carried to the ball park. And she said she would fast for him and get children to offer prayers. The next weeks he did feel a little better. So I said to myself, "Gee. Maybe . . ."

You look for help in every direction when you think there is no hope. And let's face it, as cynical as Al was, there were a few television programs with faith healers that he would ordinarily never watch, but when it was at the point of desperation as to what you are going to do next, he was watching it. He even said, "Well, . . . if this doesn't work, we'll give it a shot. We'll give it a thought."

Marty: Are there fears?

Al: Oh, there's always fear. Every day I live with fear. But it's not as strong as it was when I first got sick. I never know when I'm going to have a recurrence or when it will get worse again. Every day I feel for the tumor, which I can feel with my hand. And every day I wonder, "Is it getting any better? Is it growing? Is it getting worse?" One day it feels like it's shrinking. And then it feels twice as big. My doctor tells me he feels less of it; that it's getting softer and he's hopeful that it will eventually go away.

Marty: How has this illness affected your life together?

Al: We're closer. I think it's made us closer together, no doubt about it. We're spending more time together. In the short days I have left I want to spend more time with my little boy. I like to see him all the time. I would see him outside riding a bicycle and I would say to myself, "I don't know if I'll be seeing him next year doing this."

Marty: How do you feel your relationship with Al was affected?

Marge: Not much different. At first I was constantly worried about him. In bed at night I was afraid to move over on him. But now I continue my life as it has to be. I go to work and if I have an affair to go to in the evening, or a meeting, I will go. Before, I wouldn't go anywhere. Before, if someone came over and said, "Look. Let me take you out for dinner. You have to get out of the house," I didn't want to go—"No. I have to stay here." But now, especially when I see him looking and feeling so much better, I find that I'm right back into normal activities.

Also, it wears you out because it's so constant. I'll go hours without thinking about it, but there's not a day that doesn't go by that it doesn't cross my mind. Even now, I'll be working then all of a sudden I'll sit and my mind snaps and I'll start thinking, "Now listen. You're going to have to do this and that. Are you prepared for this? What are you going to do?" So you're always living with death. We all are. You die a little each day, every one of us. But I don't think that you or others are living with it like I am. And I hate it. I hate that horrible feeling that something else has to be oppressive on me.

As a woman, you always imagine certain things. I did, anyway. I would say, "You know, someday your husband might die." You think about it and fantasize a little bit about it. But I say I would rather have it hit me all at once, like an accident or something, and have it over than to go through this kind of a thing, really.

What helped me was the fact that I worked and wasn't just home all day. If I was home all day and always around the house, maybe things would have been more oppressive. But I was out; I talked to people. I laughed. I'd get there and people would make me laugh and I'd forget for about an hour.

Marty: Since this book will be to help people profit by others' experiences, what would you want to tell people about coping with serious illness and diagnosed fatal illness, both for those having it and those around them?

Al: That you've got to keep the faith. That you've got to have faith in your doctors, you've got to have faith in yourself, and faith in God. They all go together. It's all medicine. It's all different forms of medicine.

The doctors can only do so much for you. Your own body, your own mental attitude has to do just as much as what the doctors do for you. If you have faith and a lot of strength inside your body that you want to get well, that is like medicine and that will cure you also. That is what these faith healers do for you anyway. They psyche you up to a point where you think you're getting better, and actually you are. But if you're going to think depressed, you're going to be depressed, and your body will be depressed with it. And even though I'm not a great believer in God, I believe that there is an unknown person that is doing something either for you or against you. And you've got to have that belief that it's for your benefit that they're working. And the combination of all these things is going to help.

*   *   *

Are Al's unorthodox treatments curing him? Who knows. All one can say is that he feels better. Just as we physicians don't know what causes most cancers, neither are we certain as to what cures them.

Al's story touches areas that remain to be elaborated upon in subsequent chapters: the question of pain, of medical treatments often being more debilitating than the illness, and the needs of you, the survivor, being of particular concern. For the moment it suffices to underline the point that Al's root herbs, like Jack's diet and orgone treatments, have certainly helped sustain his hopes for however long he lives. And that, in my opinion, is sufficient—particularly when such alternative modalities of care are modestly priced, affordable, and provide a rationale for their potential effectiveness.

6

Is Pain Necessary?

("It Might Be Cancer, But I Feel Good.")

If I had the strength to hold a pen, I would write
down how easy and pleasant it is to die.
                                    —last words of William Hunter

ONE COMMONLY EXPRESSED fear of death is the fear of pain.
If there is pain in dying it is, more often than not, caused by
our doctors' attempts to retard a natural process with their
spinal taps, oxygen tents, infusions, medications, radiations,
and radical surgeries.

"Keep them alive at all costs" seems to be their motto. "Any
day now, a cure might be discovered."

There is, perhaps, no more pain in dying than in being
born, no matter how much hollering goes on in either state.
The agonies and pain that we witness in others are often per-

ceived quite differently by the sufferer than the observer. I tend
to think that the viewer exaggerates the pain. I saw this process
in action during my father's last phases of cancer.

I was with my father the night he died, holding his hand as
he lay on a bed fashioned from the living room couch, giving
him injections of morphine when his pains became intense. I
would watch the taut faces he made when the final abdominal
spasms hit, and listen to his periodic, muted screams. Yet between death seizures he told me that he felt very peaceful.
This witnessing made me realize that those watching a person
die often interpret more pain than the dying person experiences. Like watching a woman in labor, it seems dreadful to an
outsider. The mother, however, is frequently more impressed
with the excitement of the process. My father's pain seemed no
different from that. Whatever remaining fear I had of cancer
left me, and I saw that disease as no more terrifying than
any other form of death.

My father's father died of cancer, too. My grandfather was
in a hospital for about a year and so withered away that he re-
sembled those victims of starvation seen in Nazi concentration
camps. My father kept saying "I don't want to suffer like he
did."

"Did he complain?" I asked.

"No. He never complained. He was a strong person who
bore it. But you could see him suffering and wasting away."

Now, my father was making these statements when his weight
had dropped from 160 to 95 pounds. He was talking about
hoping he would not wind up like my grandfather when, to
an observer, he appeared precisely that way.

As severe as it might be, pain can almost always be controlled
with narcotics, the proper dose being the one that works.
Some doctors and even more nurses are hypnotized by standard
dosages, and resist administering prolonged and high quanti-
ties of morphine to the terminally ill. At other times, patients
themselves are reluctant to become "addicted." However, most
doctors who treat malignant diseases recognize the folly of
trying to prevent addiction in people who won't live long

enough to become hooked on drugs. It is common, nowadays, that if anyone requires one hundred milligrams of morphine each hour for relief, he or she is given that amount.

This means, of course, that if someone important to you complains that pain is severe and more medication is needed, you should urge the treating physician to accommodate the request. If the doctor is resistant to doing so, you might well consider seeing another practitioner.

More radical measures for pain relief are also available, particularly on those rare occasions when narcotics can't be used, such as cutting the sensory-nerve roots to the affected area (as was suggested to Al, before his remission).

"Most studies have shown that the gravely ill patient's greatest source of anxiety stems from being lied to and from the uncertainties that lack of candor produces," according to a leading medical oncologist, a man who treats severely ill cancer patients. His approach consists of "as much honesty and straightforwardness as the patient requires; including filling them in on every last detail if they want that." Why all the details? Because pain is highly dependent on personality factors. Small aches are magnified by the uncertainty of "What's going to happen next?" Uncertain people feel pain more. If they are informed ahead of time about the nature of their disease, its clinical course, told that distress will occur, and also given the length of time it takes to relieve suffering with medication, they seem to manage it much better.

Modern medicine's ability to greatly restrict deaths caused by ravaging infections (plague, malaria, smallpox, tuberculosis, pneumonia), its capacity to largely eliminate infant and childhood mortality, and the life-saving proficiency shown by contemporary surgeons has shifted the dying process from acute illnesses to chronic ones. Although most people still die with relative rapidity through accidents, strokes, and heart attacks, our concern here is with the increasing number of illnesses that are more drawn out, where individuals and their families have a chance to reflect upon their eventual demise.

Modern medical practice is also noted for physicians who

are often too busy to fill in patients on the details of their pathology. The following information is provided with the conviction that sharing such data means minimizing distress.

*   *   *

OVERVIEW

Death occurs when any vital organ (the brain, lungs, liver, kidney, heart, or blood) ceases to function. The process of compromising these organs produces preterminal symptoms. Obstruction of any part of the gastrointestinal system will also cause death. Though current surgical techniques can correct such abnormalities at least temporarily, one always runs the risk of death secondary to surgical complications.

No doctor can ever give a patient's exact survival time. Longevity depends on such poorly understood factors as natural resistance, highly individual responses to chemotherapy or radiotherapy, psychological makeup, and, for want of a better term, acts of God. Nevertheless, each illness does run a typical course, depending upon the organ system that is affected.

Although pain and restlessness frequently accompany the physical deterioration seen in chronic illness, the body seems to compensate for these debilitating factors shortly before death. It is a rare situation in which the end is grotesque, and most people seem quite calm before they die.

Many individuals lapse into a coma before expiring and do indeed "die in their sleep." These stuporous states are the result of liver or kidney failures or overwhelming infections (septicemia). In each of these instances, toxic products that healthy kidneys or liver tissue would ordinarily metabolize permeate the body and becloud the brain. Coma may also result from solid masses growing in the brain or from hemorrhaging into the brain tissue itself.

In addition to these natural processes, it is common medical practice to sedate the dying with high doses of phenothiazines or opiates before they enter their comatose period. This, too, eases preterminal anguish.

1) Heart disease

Two and a half times as many people die of heart disease as die of cancer. If one has a myocardial infarct (a sudden loss of blood supply to the heart itself when a coronary artery is obstructed), death can be immediate. Other cardiac illnesses are more protracted. Chronic insufficiency of the heart's blood supply caused by diseased coronary arteries produces angina and eventual scarring of the heart muscle, accompanied by its failure to circulate the blood efficiently (congestive heart failure).

Chronic congestive heart failure results in a condition known as cardiac cachexia, in which there is the wasting away (cachexia) commonly associated with cancer. Weight is maintained, though, through fluid retention, so that while muscles atrophy, the abdomen swells with fluid (*ascites*) and the extremities (hands and feet) develop pitting edema. Such patients are in respiratory trouble constantly and can barely arise from a chair without being short of breath. As with anginal conditions, there are severe chest pains. These people typically endure more pain and have a poorer prognosis than most cancer conditions cause, yet they are not nearly as afraid of their condition as they would be of having a malignancy. For a variety of reasons, cancer poses a greater psychological threat, the foreign invader that eats you up being much more frightening than a debilitated heart.

In final failure there is great restlessness, associated with the inability to ventilate adequately as the lungs fill with fluid. This respiratory insufficiency often causes a carbon dioxide narcosis that can be very helpful for its calming effect. Death usually results from cardiac collapse, as the progressively anoxic heart muscles eventually fail to keep blood pulsing through overloaded circuits.

2) Blood

Hematological tumors (blood cancers, such as the leukemias and lymphomas) have much more frequent remissions than do solid tumors. (Breast cancer is the exception, women with widespread breast cancer being known to live for ten years with different treatments.) Eventual death from blood disease is usually the result'of bleeding or infections. Hemorrhaging occurs throughout the body; in such instances, blood cannot be replaced fast enough. This leads to circulatory collapse, shock, and death. Frequently there is terminal bleeding into the brain, which produces coma and a reasonably painless death.

Perhaps 60 percent of patients with blood disorders die of infection (as do a high percentage of all cancer patients, for the drugs used to kill tumor cells also destroy the white blood cells that ordinarily combat bacterial and viral diseases). This sepsis (infection throughout the body) may be quite unpleasant, causing high temperatures, sweating, and the overall aching that accompanies severe sickness, but is short lived, since the toxins produced by the invading pathogens soon result in exhaustion and loss of contact. This stage, which is without suffering, may go on for days before one lapses into coma and death.

3) Gastrointestinal system

The symptoms of gastrointestinal disease vary, but consist usually of abdominal pain, nausea, vomiting, and bleeding into the gastrointestinal tract which manifests itself in black stools or bright blood in the vomitus or the feces. The course and prognosis of cancerous growths depend upon where the riginal lesion occurred. Cancer of the colon (large intestine), even when surgically incurable, may be successfully held in check for years with currently available drugs. Stomach cancer has a more rapid downhill course. Ultimately, both forms end up metastasizing to the liver, causing liver failure, or obstruction of the bowel or gall bladder, requiring surgical intervention. Death finally results from surgery, liver failure, or infection.

4) Kidneys

Advanced kidney disease such as chronic glomerulonephritis

(or the extremely sluggish circulation seen in congestive heart failure) causes a build-up of urea (a toxin) in the blood-stream, as it cannot be efficiently excreted. As the blood urea nitrogen level (BUN) elevates, its poisonous effects are seen in shortness of breath, disorientation, lack of appetite, general wasting, bone demineralization (resulting in fractures from minor injuries), nausea, vomiting, hiccups, itching, nose bleeds (as clotting is inhibited), restlessness, and muscular twitching. Stupor, coma, and death follow from these circulating metabolic waste products. Death may also result from massive bleeding into the brain.

5) Liver

The liver transforms all foodstuffs, digested and absorbed in the intestines, into material the body needs to sustain itself. It has so many major metabolic functions—from protein, carbohydrate, and lipid metabolism, to enzyme production and synthesis of blood-clotting factors—that extensive illness produces a multiplicity of chemical deficiencies and toxins that are inimical to life.

Symptoms of disease are similar to those of gastrointestinal disturbances, but include as well jaundice, bleeding tendencies, upper abdominal pains, headaches, and abnormal reflexes. Ascites results from the failure of intestinal blood to pass readily through the liver tissue. This blockage causes a build-up of venous blood pressure and may result in massive esophageal bleeding and hemorrhoidal bleeding, a common cause of death in the case of cirrhosis.

Hepatic pre-coma, brought about by accumulated toxins, causes disorientation and drowsiness. These same substances, shortly before death, produce coma and a sharp rise in temperature. Expiration is frequently the result of massive hemorrhaging.

6) Lungs

Coughing, chest pains, pleural effusions (fluid in the chest cavity), and pulmonary edema (fluid in the air sacs) all contribute to eventual dyspnea (air hunger), which can cause great discomfort. Respiratory insufficiency may lead to a calming carbon-dioxide narcosis, as occurs in congestive heart failure.

The average life span of diagnosed untreatable carcinoma of the lung is nine months, but survival for two years or more is not uncommon. Metastatic disease in the lungs has a shorter prognosis. Primary lung carcinomas commonly produce the hormone ACTH, which stimulates the adrenal gland to manufacture excess cortisone. This is another example of the way the body makes death easier, for cortisone generates a feeling of euphoria. Death is preceded by lethargy, disorientation, lack of appetite, and coma.

7) Brain

The brain stem contains vital centers that regulate heartbeat, respiration, and hormonal activity. Destruction of this area of the brain makes survival impossible.

Brain involvement from cancer is mainly metastatic, but whether primary or from another source, there is no typical course. It depends, instead, upon the area of the brain involved. This determines whether one has symptoms of speech defects, balance and walking problems, or impairment of sight. Headaches and personality changes may also occur.

8) Prostatic cancer

The prostate gland surrounds the neck of the bladder. The initial symptom of cancer is akin to that of benign enlargement: urinary retention. Malignancies, however, soon spread to the bones, are often quite painful, and cause pathological fractures.

In 1966, Charles Huggins received a Nobel Prize for discovering that prostatic malignancies are under the control of the sex hormones. Current treatment, when there is bone involvement, consists of orchiectomy (removal of the testes), since testosterone stimulates tumor growth, along with administration of estrogen, which retards it. From the day of orchiectomy, bone pain literally halts and complete remission, free of pain, often lasts for two or three years. Eventually the tumor escapes the control of the hormones, and pains return. Secondary drug treatment is less successful. The tumor then crowds out the bone marrow and the patient can't make enough red cells and platelets, causing death from anemia, bleeding, or both. A concomitant depression of white-cell production can result in death from infection.

9) *Breast, Ovarian, and Uterine Cancers*

Great advances in the drug treatment of breast cancer have meant that women who are not cured surgically and develop metastatic disease can have their life span appreciably prolonged. Newer drugs can induce remissions in more than 50 percent of women. A third of breast tumors are also susceptible to hormone treatment which, as in prostatic cancer, can add significant longevity.

Preterminal symptoms and the actual cause of death depend on the site of major metastasis. Breast tumors may go anywhere, particularly to bone (where pain is greatest), the brain, liver, or lungs.

Uterine tumors are similar to breast cancer insofar as treatment procedures are concerned. These are much less common diseases, usually metastasizing to the lung or liver, and cause less pain.

Ovarian malignancies are often not diagnosed until it is too late for corrective surgery. Ascites and wasting are common, and death often follows an infection that the debilitated person cannot shake off.

10) *Other Chronic Diseases*

There are a host of chronic illnesses that are also life threatening. The time they take to do their damage is not, however, as limited as in most cases of severe heart diseases or cancer.

Thus, sufferers of these diseases do not usually have to confront their own mortality as decisively or abruptly.

a) *Diabetes* and *hypertension* are two common examples of such chronic illnesses. Many patients are maintained for decades relatively symptom-free. Both of these maladies have long-term effects on the heart and blood vessels. When it occurs, death is usually through myocardial infarcts (heart attacks), congestive heart failure, strokes, and renal (kidney) failure.

b) Collagen disorders such as *amyloidosis* and other inflammatory processes, like *systemic lupus erythematosis,* are illnesses of unknown origin and vague symptomatology. Both are suspected to result from an allergic reaction gone haywire. Substances are produced which invade and compromise the various organs. The courses of these sicknesses are irregular and marked by remissions and exacerbations. During the acute and/or final phases, the problems faced depend on the organs most affected. These are usually the kidney, heart, or liver.

3) Neuromuscular diseases such as *multiple sclerosis* (a degenerative disorder of the central nervous system), *amyotrophic lateral sclerosis* (the paralyzing, spinal-cord sickness that felled Lou Gehrig), or the inherited *muscular dystrophy* are similarly marked by periodic recurrences and disappearance of symptoms. Lack of coordination, tremors, weakness, and visual disturbances are common. Death often results from overwhelming infections that follow general, eventual debilitation.

One could go on endlessly listing the various esoteric diseases that do humans in. Suffice it to say that they all have a common ending, regardless of their different causalities. Terminal symptoms, once more, relate to the vital organs that are eventually affected.

*   *   *

The pain involved in a life-threatening illness is a highly personal response and is tolerated differently by each individual. As anyone who has gone to the dentist knows, the anticipation of suffering is often far worse than the suffering itself. Pain does pass, although worries about it may linger. People frequently endure grave illnesses and much surgery, yet they have few physical complaints.

Lillian is a sixty-eight-year-old woman with metastatic lung cancer. Problems in ambulating and balance caused her hospitalization. Her story demonstrates how the body frequently compensates for disease processes in ways that minimize pain.

Cancerous cells spread to her brain and produced excess ACTH, a hormone which stimulates the production of cortisone. The cortisone accounted for her moon-shaped face, and its euphoric effect also spared Lilly the physical pain that another malignancy might have caused.

Alert and lively and wearing a print dress, she has just returned to her hospital bed after spending the morning in the eye clinic, where she went for a cataract checkup. Her voice sounds like a Yiddish Gracie Allen; her attitude is akin to Mel Brooks's two-thousand-year-old man. She is a small woman with thin white hair and blue eyes which peer from behind the strongest bifocals I've ever seen.

Lilly died peacefully two weeks after our meeting. She was a very remarkable and likable lady.

Lilly: I was down there so long, it's hard to believe. How long was I down there? Two hours?

Marty: It's a long time. Hospitals mean waiting and waiting and waiting.

Lilly: I'll never forget, I needed a bed pan once. They didn't give it to me right away, and that's something you've got to have. You just can't wait. I used to have it over here (gestures to side of bed). I said, "This is my security blanket." Because I need it. You never know.

Now that I learned to go down from the bed, I don't mind it that much. Only at night I don't want to take a chance because I can't see too well. But by day, thank God, I got better. I was a vegetable.

Marty: You were . . .

Lilly: [definitely] I *was* a vegetable.

Marty: How long ago was that?

Lilly: I lost count because I was in the hospital for a checkup and they sent me to a convalescent home. It wasn't for me. The youngest person there was eighty-one. They kept running to the beauty parlor, but I lost the power of my legs. I started to get very sick, and they brought me back here.

Marty: What is your illness that is causing these things?

Lilly: Well, I was supposed to go for a cataract. I had a glaucoma operation. That was more than a year ago. And when they started checking—they don't operate right away—they take X rays here, they take X rays there. Anyway, they found something wrong in the lung. They took out a tumor and part of my lung. I was fine after that.

Marty: You didn't have any symptoms at all?

Lilly: No. Just the cataracts. I never complained. I walked for miles. I was a very, very strong woman. I had nothing wrong with me.

Marty: You never smoked?

Lilly: Oh! I smoked a lot! The smoking didn't bother me.

Marty: What was a lot? A pack a day?

Lilly: Well, over a pack. I used to go to sleep late, and I'd open a second pack.

Marty: For many years?

Lilly: For many years? Oh, my God, for half my life. (She lights a cigarette.) But that didn't bother me. I didn't cough. After the operation, I asked the doctor. I said, "I can't just stop." So he said, "Go ahead." So the smoking didn't bother me at all. I was fine after the operation. I had pipes, pipes, pipes all over me, thick pipes like this over here. (Gestures to her arms, lower abdomen, chest, nose.) When they took the pipes out I got out of bed and walked to the bathroom. So that operation didn't bother me at all. I never had pain.

Marty: And you don't have pain now, either?

Lilly: No. And it still isn't healed. See, it's healed on the outside, but here (moves hand over chest wall) there is still a feeling of numbness.
  But a couple of weeks ago I twisted my back, and, oh my, it was painful. Anyway, I didn't feel so good. I finally got very tired, and I went to the doctor, and he said that he wanted me to go into the hospital for a checkup because I have pebbles over here (again points to her chest wall). So they took that out. And there's something wrong with my liver. But I never complained. I've never had any pain since I'm sick.

Marty: I don't know how much your doctor talked to you about what I'm doing, but I'm writing a book about life-threatening illnesses, and . . .

Lilly: There's something wrong with me. I can guess it, you know what I mean?

Marty: Guessing in terms of what?

Lilly: Wel-l-l-l. Cancer. I don't know.

Marty: Nobody ever told you the diagnosis, so you don't really know what's wrong with you?

Lilly: And I don't want to know. I don't care. At my age, I don't care no more. I'll be sixty-nine in March. So-o-o . . .

Marty: So you don't care whether it's serious or not. Whatever happens, happens.

Lilly [bouncily]: Whatever happens! Look. You can't take life in your own hands.

Marty: But you think it might be cancer.

Lilly: I have a feeling. They never told me. But I feel good. My operation didn't bother me. I never had any pain.

Marty: So cancer's not so bad?

Lilly: Well, the doctor's controlling something with the blood, I know. When I came in the second time . . . the medication they gave me for the liver, see—I lost all my hair. He gave me an injection and he told me, "It's going to happen." [Laughs.] But I didn't believe that, and boy, I lost it. And now [enthusiastically] it's growing in.

Marty: It must be hard for a woman to lose her hair at any age.

Lilly: Oh, my God. I was furious. The medication that he gave me for the liver did something to my white blood. I was bad. I had a lot of fever.

Marty: But you never asked your doctor what your sickness was about? You never wanted to know?

Lilly: I gave him a hint and that's enough.

Marty: What was the hint?

Lilly: Well, I told him, "I know what I've got." I didn't come out with it, but I said it, like that. And he [she makes an on-and-off motion with her hand] went "Mmmmmmm," you know?

Marty: He said "Yes?"

Lilly: It sounded like. So I really don't know, and I don't care. I got to the stage where I don't care.

Marty: Okay. Because I could find out. I could just go outside and look at the chart.

Lilly: [her eyes sparkling conspiratorially]: Go ahead. [then, quickly, and loudly] Nah. Nah, darling.

Marty: You don't want me to.

Lilly: Nah. It's not necessary.

Marty: You'd rather be in for a surprise.

Lilly: No. It'll come. Let it just come slowly. I don't want to know. If it is, it is. If it isn't, it isn't. I don't really care.

Marty: You're a very lively woman. You're full of life.

Lilly: I am!! I was!! I used to walk—you know, before coming here, before getting sick—I live on Madison Street. You know where Madison Street is? All the way downtown near the East River. I walked from there to 63rd Street and Lexington Avenue. It's a big, big walk. And then I walked all the way up to Seventh Avenue, the same day. Slowly I strutted, like, and then walked all the way back to 34th Street and Second Avenue, and then I took the bus home.

Marty: Do you have a lot of relatives who come in?

Lilly: Wel-l-l-l, my sister and two nieces, my children, my grandchildren.

Marty: And how do they treat you when you're sick?

Lilly: How do they treat me? [chuckles] They come to see me.

Marty: The same as always. What did you do? What kind of work?

Lilly [a little ashamedly]: Oh. Very dirty work. I used to clean offices. They used to say I didn't look it. And I used to say, "Well, I don't have to advertise my profession." I used to come dressed up and I'd have different clothes to change to there. It was honest work, but of course, I wasn't educated and that's what happened.

Marty: Are you a religious lady?

Lilly [defiantly]: No.

Marty: An atheist?

Lilly: No.

Marty: An agnostic?

Lilly: Whatever you call it. I'm honest. My heart is good. My religion is in my heart. I never insulted anybody. I never cursed anybody. I was never jealous of anybody. So to me that's my religion.

Marty: That's nice. I like that for an idea of religion.

Lilly: That's mine. And always, all the years, I never in my life had a fight with anybody. 'Cause when I see somebody that is not too smart, I don't want to win. So I walk away. It's crazy [laughs] but that's what I do.

Marty: You really think that's crazy? Or are you proud of it?

Lilly: I am proud of it. I don't know how other people think, but I'm proud of it. I'm talking into this [microphone]. Can I hear it back? [I play the tape back. She doesn't think it sounds like her.]

I used to sing Jewish songs. I try to remember. When I was sick I'd lay in bed and think of those songs. It's crazy.

Marty: It's crazy to lay in bed and think of songs?

Lilly: Yes. To *sing* while you're laying there, in the hospital. [laughs.]

Marty: But you're cheery.

Lilly: I am, I am. My whole life. Thank God for that. I used to make everybody laugh.

Marty: What do you look forward to in the future?

Lilly: Not a thing bothers me. I'm thinking *now*.

Marty: So you don't know what you'll do when you leave. You'll think of that then.

Lilly: I don't know whether I'll get out on the street. I have a flight of steps to walk up. That's the trouble. Otherwise I never think ahead. I live now.

*   *   *

Is pain necessary?

Between the natural responses of the body and the power-ful suppressant powers of narcotics, the answer is an emphatic No!

7

Helping Out

*Michele Murray is not listed in the highest ranks of American letters—her rise was prevented by many forces —but for a group of her followers she was unique as a human being and as an artist. She died, at forty, tormented by cancer, her death coming in her home with her husband offering final mercies and thoughts. The last hours of her life, amid her family and the books of

*This excerpt is from the essay "On the Death of a Young Poet" by Colman McCarthy, which appeared in the Washington *Post*, March 19, 1974.
© Washington *Post*.

her home library where she studied and wrote, were a stirring resistance against the tyranny of death. Perhaps if she had died the conventional American death—stuck in a hospital room, ministered to by strangers, and kept from knowing the end was coming—many of those who knew her would not now be thinking that her life and ideas also had special meaning. The beauty of her death called out for reflections on the beauty of her life and writing.

On the morning of the day before she died, Mrs. Murray, lying on a small couch in her library, talked individually with three of her four children—David, eighteen; Jonathan, sixteen; and Sarah, thirteen. She told them she would die soon, though she didn't know when, and that she had enjoyed being their mother. And she offered, characteristically, practical advice about their lives after her death. She had a comfortable day, however, and a comfortable night as well.

But by 10 A.M. the next day, she began losing consciousness. Her husband Jim read her the joyful psalms and the poetry of Catherine de Vinck, played recordings of Mozart's chamber music for her, kissed her and prayed with her. Between one and two in the afternoon, she died.

At three in the afternoon, the two oldest children came home from school, and the father took them in to see the body of their mother. One son, with skills in drawing, closed the door and sketched a picture. Americans have been conditioned to avoid even thinking about death, much less looking at it, but for months this one family had been gently coached by its father, with its dying mother's tacit agreement, not to hide from death when it came. "There is growth in silence," she had written in her journal.

The serenity of Michele Murray's death was made possible by an open attitude within her family, by the apparent willingness of each member of it to communicate truthfully, and by their availability.

Helpfulness is a two-way street. By confronting death candidly and naturally, this wife and mother dispelled dread of the unnameable in those she cared for. By sharing her thoughts and feelings with her husband and children, she helped them to do the same with her. Having worked through her own anxieties and sorrows, she set an example for them, too, one day to die with grace, compassion, and understanding.

And how did those who love her help? By sitting silently, by being available to talk, to listen, to touch, to share.

For both the ill and the well, the ultimate task is to arrive at a final state of acceptance—for the dying to die with dignity and for the living to meet the challenges of an altered way of life. One cannot either live or die in comfort and at peace if one is worried, preoccupied, isolated, or uncertain. Dispelling such interfering emotions represents our major task.

> Dying is ceasing to be afraid.
> —William Wycherley

A stoic's mask—the calm, silent face that hides gnawing doubts—will not do. Worries have a way of abating when they are shared and expressed, as do grief and anger. Unspoken feelings and unmade decisions often cause additional anguish retrospectively. If ever there was a time for people to have honest and trustworthy communications with one another, the period preceding death ranks first in importance. This is the last opportunity one has to truly share another's soul; their perspectives, philosophies, loves, and longings. To let it pass is perhaps the ultimate tragedy in death, more so than death itself. Death we can do nothing about, but meaningful communication is within the power of each of us.

What we communicate about will, of course, depend on our own thoughts and on those of the dying. These will vary greatly from one individual to another and will also change over the course of time. Two determining factors relate to the age of the ill person and to the stage of dying they are in.

Before the age of five, for instance, most children think of death as a reversible process. Just as a bulb, buried in the earth, might bloom into a plant the following spring, so might a buried person reemerge. Such concepts account for unique fears and unique tranquilities in the face of death. And these, along with concern about the possibility of damage being done to a rapidly growing and ever-more-skillfully functioning body, are subjects that are likely to be expressed.

In later childhood, death is often related to punishment, or to getting love one otherwise wouldn't. It still remains a riddle, for one's experience and exposure are limited.

Adolescence offers an opportunity to enter into a totally new world, and a teen-ager is particularly apt to feel cheated knowing that he or she won't live long enough to experience it. Thomas' admonition—"Do not go gentle into that good night/Rage, rage against the dying of the light"—is a natural response at this age where one is aware of potentials and deeply resentful of limitations.

Concepts like "don't wed too young," "don't have kids before you can afford them," and "don't travel about until you finish your education" have haunted many young adults and add up to "Don't live in the present, but prepare for a better tomorrow instead." Little wonder that death, at this age, continues to be perceived as a threat, with its potential to terminate aspirations prematurely and to render life incomplete.

By the thirties and forties, most people have fulfilled as well as they can their earlier goals. Death anxiety then tends to shift from self to others. Many observers have repeatedly noted that death is hardest to accept among those who leave dependent children behind them. A feeling of letting down young survivors replaces one of being personally cheated.

Middle age, the mid-forties and fifties, is often accompanied by feelings that life's options are limited, that one has exhausted the possibilities of fulfillment in love and work. Associates begin to die at ever-increasing rates. And those who make it to old age, the sixties and seventies, are constantly reminded by aching bodies and actuarial tables that their time is imminent. There are worries about pain, loneliness, or being a burden on or beholden to others. Many simply bide their time, confined within withering bodies, awaiting release from a tedious existence.

These are the age-related themes you might expect to hear; the responses encountered during the various decades of life. There are other themes that occur during the days, weeks, and months following the realization that one is fatally ill. Dr. Kübler-Ross, whose experience with the dying exceeds that of any other observer I've come across, describes five stages that terminally sick people typically go through, stages that invariably overlap.

Stage One is Denial and Isolation. "It can't be me. . . . It must be a mistake. . . . I'll consult another doctor." These are common responses to grave diagnoses as the ill person hopes to deny the reality of the situation.

Stage Two, Anger, comes with the recognition that a fatal prognosis is indeed correct. Envy may be felt toward the living. This is the "Why me?" stage. Resentments are projected out into the surrounding environment. Doctors, nurses, and family are reacted to with irritation or bitterness while the individual expresses his frustration and mobilizes his rage as an antagonist against death.

Stage Three, Bargaining, follows when anger futilely spends itself. Just as children try to get their way by good behavior, after unsuccessfully railing against a parental limitation, one holds counsel with God to postpone the ultimate finality. "If you let me live to see my son's graduation I'll dedicate my life to you . . . give my body to science . . . never be curt with my mother-in-law again."

Stage four is Depression. Disbelief, anger, and bargaining have failed to reverse the sequence of events. Further hospitalizations, surgery, and treatments cause discomfort and add financial stress. There is a reaction to past losses as well as anticipated future loss. A preparatory grief naturally follows all these events. At this time, one deals with the sadness of realizing that final good-byes to the familiar world are in order, that particularly pleasurable moments and friends will not be experienced again.

Stage Five, Acceptance, is arrived at when the other feelings are expressed and spent. Unfinished business is completed, there is little physical pain, and there is a great feeling of peace. There is neither depression nor anger, and death comes to be viewed as a release.

> First our pleasures die—and then
> Our hopes, and then our fears—and when
> These are dead, the debt is due,
> Dust claims dust—and we die too.
> —Percy Bysshe Shelley

Acceptance of death on everyone's part is facilitated when there is ample opportunity for the expression of thoughts and feelings. Both the living and the dying need to transcend denial, resentments, and depression in order to get on with their respective tasks. You must learn to tolerate such feelings without trying to talk people out of them, if you are to be helpful. We habitually try to cheer up sad people. Yet, to tell a dying man in the final phases of disease that he ought to pay attention to the sunnier side of life denies him the opportunity to contemplate and finally accept death. Parting from all that is familiar, from loved associates and from one's own self, is naturally sad, and this sadness ought to be expressed and respected. The placebo effect of false optimism becomes a bitter pill when hope is unrealized. The sense of betrayal that follows the dashing of such hopes is not the road to acceptance.

> Although you want to last forever
> You know you never will
> And good-byes make the journey harder
> still.
> —Cat Stevens

If you can help a dying adolescent to say "Why me? Why so young?" you have done enough. We needn't give answers, provide palliatives or play God. It is sufficient simply to help the other person express their sentiments.

One helps, also, by ending feelings of obligation. The dying often feel obliged to live on, by relatives who either can't face their passing or feel morally bound to keep them alive. Told to fight it and hang in there, the moribund are torn between quiet acceptance of death as inevitable, and feelings of guilt and remorse for letting their dependents down.

Ultimately, there are two viable options, not mutually exclusive, to take toward death. One consists of passive acceptance, the other being an active struggling against it. Those who have shared their lives within these pages have demonstrated both reactions. They accept, but also hope to prolong their time on earth.

It is infinitely more difficult for relatives to "accept the dying person's acceptance" than it is to support their will to live. We survivors invariably feel obliged to care for those who don't seem to care about themselves. We urge all sorts of moderation and precautions upon them, not recognizing that every individual has a right to live and die in his or her own way. In fact, we cannot help those who are either bent on self-destruction or are willing simply to abandon the flesh. Nor need we feel guilty for failing.

Bill is a close friend of mine. Forty-seven-years-old, of black, white, and Hawaiian ancestry, he is very much a self-made man. A street fighter when he was younger, he was constantly in trouble with the law. After several jailings he put himself through college, became a social worker, and dedicated himself to helping the children of the ghettos. Brawny, scarred, broken knuckled and barrel chested, he was one of the strongest men I'd ever encountered.

Two years ago he impoverished himself by securing the best care he could for his mother after she suffered a stroke. One year ago he was stricken with unexplainable lung congestion and was immediately hospitalized. Recently the diagnosis became clear. He suffers from amyloidosis involving the heart muscles. There have been two episodes of congestive heart failure since then.

I visited him at the hospital on the second occasion. He was propped up in bed in an oxygen tent, had an intravenous going, was wheezing, and in great respiratory distress. Yet his demeanor was calm and cheerful. Following that episode, his condition stabilized. Although he has been discharged from in-patient care, his prognosis is poor.

Bill knows what he faces, and is quite accepting of death, to the consternation of many people who care about him. But if we see things through his eyes, perhaps we'll be more tolerant when someone we know experiences a similar acceptance.

*   *   *

Bill: The whole concept that I was going to die had built up from about nine months prior to my first hospitalization. I had told Helen to be prepared. I was in the process of making a will, splitting things up between Helen, my ex-wife, and mother, when I had this premonition that I was going to die from a sudden heart attack.

I felt that I was into a groovy space prior to my becoming ill. I had made connections to all the beautiful people in my life that I had injured and it was time for me to leave. The reason for that is that I fully believe in reincarnation. I feel that I have reached a point in my life where I'm coming back as a better person. As for dying, I felt I had some control over it. I knew what was going down with me and I could say, "Hey, let it happen."

Marty: When you felt you were on the point of death and had that oxygen hunger, what were your feelings? Both what you felt in your body and your mental attitude?

Bill: My body said, "Man, I'm going. But I hate having all this damn pain." These people sticking all these needles in me. The needles just blew me away. There was something of a need for me to survive which was being supported by them, and there was something of a need for me to die, which was my thing. I was very ambivalent about it all the time. There were certain times where the needle broke free from my neck. I woke up on three occasions where it came out and I could have died in my sleep, because the blood was just gushing all over the place. That I would die without having said good-bye to the people I wanted to say good-bye to was the funniest feelings; that although Helen knew it, I didn't get a chance to say good-bye to her and to some others. There were people who were important to me at that time. I wanted to say good-bye to the world through them, and then do my own thing and come back in a different space.

I believe that if I put more energy into it, I could really survive. But I don't want to put that much energy into it. For some reason or other I'm not willing to do that.

Marty: You had a faith in reincarnation even before your difficulties.

Bill: Yes. I had.

Marty: And how are you feeling now?

Bill: I do feel weak, but better than I felt at the time.
My body may be going down, but my mind is expanding. I

no longer care to the degree that I cared about people. I'm no longer that sensitized. I'm into my own thing. It's a whole head thing, a higher consciousness trip.

I feel I'm at peace with myself now. I notice that another change came over me in the hospital. I'm not as grooved in to people as I used to be. I used to give a lot of energy to people, being extremely sensitive to their needs. Very caring and very concerned about them.

Marty: You're less sensitive to people now?

Bill: Yes. I retreat into my own place. I want my privacy. Even with you. There was a time I would jump and go someplace because Marty would want to go there. Now it's because I would want to do it. If you hadn't wanted to talk now, at this time when I'm available, I wouldn't be here.

And I'm getting more enemies. I say to them, "That's your bag. Because you have expectancies of the way you saw Bill—the giving type of person all the time." That's one factor in my wanting to stay around, playing in my own space for my own self rather than doing for others. Because that's what happened to my old man and that's what happened to my mother. My father used to spend all his money for other people. That's why we never had anything. My mother was always doing good, and that's what caused her stroke.

Marty: And this came to you in the hospital.

Bill: That's right. I received over four-hundred-some-odd letters there, and I wrote to just about everybody who sent me a letter. And I thanked each visitor personally. While I could easily get into a bag of being thankful for these people who are sharing my time, I'm really not that thankful. They did it because they wanted to. Not because they had to.

The most interesting thing for me is that I'm ready to die at any time. I used to worry that I'd die by hanging or the electric chair because of my attitudes of doing people in and messing people up. But I'm not in that space now.

Marty: It sounds very beautiful. It sounds like since you're prepared to die at any time you're living more fully now.

Bill: I am. And willing to let people live more fully. I've overcome a controlling factor in me that people have to be the way I want them to be. And that's what's also made me mellower.

Marty: How long do you think you're going to live? Any estimates for yourself?

Bill: I'm not sure. I wanted to know what was happening, how close to death I was, and the doctor said, "You can go at any time. You can live a month or a year or five years."

Years ago it would have bugged me, because I really wanted to have that control. But now I know that whatever's going to happen to me is going to happen to me.

Marty: Do people get upset that you don't take better care of yourself?

Bill: Yes. Particularly people in Helen's consciousness-raising group who have been supportive to me the whole time. They mother me. And I tell them, "I'm doing my own thing. If I happen to die right now, it's because I took responsibility for being where I am." So they get upset. My father says he accepts it, but in the letters that he writes to me he gets upset. And my father and I have never been that close.

Marty: Is it very hard for you, feeling that they are trying to make you toe the line 100 percent?

Bill: At times. And I revolt and flash in their faces what I'm going to do. Like with you at times. You tell me not to smoke and I think, "Hell, it's my body and I'll do with it what I wish." I know that something better is going to happen to it. It's not going to be worse, but better.

*   *   *

Survivors often feel obliged to eat, sleep, and work death; to be constantly at the fatally ill person's bedside and never to laugh, amuse, or otherwise divert themselves. But one needs a break from such constant pressure. The time of someone's dying ought also to be a time when future survivors establish new contacts with the outer world. One needs time off, as well, for one's own peace of mind if one is to go back again and comfort the sick.

As dying lingers on, attending family members often feel that all would be better off if it were done with. Such common reactions can also be burdensome and provoke guilt. These thoughts, too, are best shared, along with the indefinable guilt that something you did or failed to do prevented successful treatment of the disease in the first place.

Again and again, I return to the theme of open and honest communication as the most useful element in helping someone to die in comfort and dignity. Failure to communicate honestly not only prevents full sharing of thoughts and feelings but deprives everyone of an opportunity to plan for the future (see Chapter 11, *Planning Ahead*). This deprivation, in effect, renders life meaningless before it is even over. The ill person is killed psychologically before biological processes cease.

So much depends on availability, on spending sufficient time with the dying person and being willing to hear them out. For instance, listen to the young mother of a leukemic son, who after a year of therapy with Kübler-Ross felt comfortable enough to stop giving her son false reassurances and instead engage in the following dialogue with her child:

> "Mommy, this time I feel so sick I think I'm going to die," he said during her visit to the hospital.
> "What do you think is going to happen?" his mother asked.
> "I think an ambulance will take me to a cemetery where Beth-Ann [a deceased friend] is."
> "Anything else I should know?"

"Yes. Tell the doctor to put the lights on and sound the alarm very loudly so Beth-Ann knows I'm coming."

Being available means a willingness to sit quietly with someone for periods of time. It means communicating with touches and gestures. It indicates an openness to share the concerns and interests of the dying. When I visited my father in the hospital or his home, we were just there, with and for one another, without an agenda or any pressure to speak about or avoid anything. At times we'd say nothing and just drift in and out of our own reveries. Or we might talk of my family, share some jokes we'd heard, speak about his illness, watch the New York Knicks play basketball on television, and say how we felt about each other. There was a natural flow about all this. We neither wallowed in melancholy nor engaged in diversions. Instead, we shared our moment-to-moment concerns and curiosities, our time and our responses. It was this focus in here-and-now processes that made this a time of intense living for both of us.

Helpfulness may also mean acting as an advocate for those you love in speaking with their doctors, in seeing to it that their priorities are put before those of the physician, that they receive truthful reports, adequate medication, and home treatment (as opposed to hospitalization or office visits) if they so desire.

Help can also be extended to survivors. Baby-sitting for small children while wives visit husbands in the hospital, preparing meals for those who are spending time with the dying, or taking them out for an evening of diversion are concrete actions that are greatly appreciated. These acts are more immediate and more helpful than words of condolence or vague offers to "call me if you need anything."

"But the most important thing," says Kübler-Ross, "is to live today and love and let people know that you love them so there are no regrets tomorrow. If you tell someone 'I love you' when they can hear you, you can keep all the schmaltzy eulogies afterwards."

8

It's Harder for the Family

KAREN IS A twenty-seven-year-old nurse, married for two and a half years, who was diagnosed fifteen months ago as having Hodgkin's disease, a malignancy of the lymph nodes.

A soft-spoken woman with dark black hair, delicate features, and expressive eyes, standing just over five feet tall, she has been on both sides of the doctor-patient relationship. Thus, she has been in a unique position to discover what medical personnel don't know about the subjective feelings of the seriously ill.

Her story documents several points already made and some

that will be elaborated upon in future chapters: of the difficulty of not knowing, of passing through the stages of dying that Kübler-Ross described, of how medical treatments are often more painful and terrifying than the disease itself, and of the desirability of post-mortem planning.

More than any of the other interviewees, Karen focuses on the problem of dying from the perspective of the family. Her great sensitivity, curiosity, practicality, and compassion stand as strong and worthy models. Would that all of us attain the same level of consciousness and be prepared to live and die as well.

*   *   *

Karen: I think it is harder for the family to adjust to a death than for the individual who is dying. The sick person receives the care and concern of the family, and relatives are told, "You have to do this and that for so and so. You must not change anything. Just make her happy." And the husband, mother, father, sit there, completely isolated, and don't really have a chance to say how they feel. I think a very good doctor, which we have, will sit down with the family and get at their feelings about the situation.

I had a roommate, a young girl, thirty-four-years-old, with a very rare type of uterine cancer. She is now doing very well, but they don't know how long this will last. She had cobalt therapy. Her husband [they have four children] is not very mature to begin with, but the end result of no one talking to him is that he tried to kill himself a few months ago. He said he could not take it any longer. Being told that he had to be strong for Liz, that he had to take care of the boys, that he had to do everything, he said, "The hell with it. I don't want to do this anymore." Liz had adjusted extremely well. She is going to graduate from nursing school in two weeks.

The patient is the first one, in the majority of cases, to come to grips with the diagnosis. It is much harder for the family.

When I was in the hospital, the oncologist on my case told

my husband that I would be dead in three montns. didn't know this. This was an additional strain on my husband who, when I wanted to talk to him about my illness, would draw away from me. This too is a very common thing. Yet I feel I am not more terminal than you are. Everybody is terminally ill, but some are terminally ill faster than others.

Marty: How many months ago did they tell him that?

Karen: Fourteen. A lot of times doctors say things which are infuriating. When I had trouble with my chemotherapy and was vomiting constantly, I asked this first oncologist, "Why don't you give me some Tigan or Compazine or something like that?" And he said, "It won't work." I said, "Prove to me it won't work. Just don't be a defeatest about it." But I was fit to be tied. I said, "Don't talk to me like there is no hope, that there is no reason to try these various things. I am willing to try Tigan. If it doesn't work I will try Compazine. If they don't work I will take Dramamine. I will try them all. But don't say to me it is not going to work."

Marty: When did you first feel ill?

Karen: Officially I knew about it September fifth, 1973. I had called my brother, a physician, about two months before that and told him that I had Hodgkin's disease. "All you nurses are alike," he said. "You all become hypochrondriacs." I don't see my brother very often, so he didn't see what I looked like. I had lost weight. I never weighed much, but I had gone from ninety-six pounds (which I am now) down to eighty, and eventually got as low as seventy-three. There were so many things indicative of Hodgkin's disease—the itching, fevers in the afternoon. I had narrowed it down to tuberculosis, Hodgkin's disease, lymphosarcoma, or an acute case of hypochondria. It had to be one of the four. But still, as sure as I was that it was Hodgkin's, like a lot of other people I wouldn't go to the doctor. It got to the point where I was passing out in the bank or I'd be taking a shower and feel like I would pass out or kill myself falling. Then I went into the university hospital for a possible ectopic pregnancy.

It wasn't that at all. While I was there, they did a sedimentation rate [an indicator of chronic diseases] and found it at a ridiculously high 280, and a hematocrit which showed a severe anemia. Then I was sure it was Hodgkin's. I knew then that I was in pretty bad shape, but I didn't go for a check-up because I didn't want to be told, finally, that that was what it was.

As a nurse I'd get angry with patients when they'd say "I found a lump a year ago, but I didn't want to go for an examination." Now I understand that it is very difficult to bring yourself to that final "Yes, it is," or "No, it isn't." Especially when you're so sure it's going to be "Yes, it is." Finally, this doctor who I had worked with at the hospital admitted me for a work-up. I had said to him several months before that I thought I had Hodgkin's disease, but he wanted so much to believe that that was not what it was that I went through every test in the book before they finally decided to do the biopsy and confirm it.

The biopsy was done in the morning and I was awake shortly after surgery, but he didn't come into my room. This was not like him at all. That is also how I knew how I was doing, as far as my tests went. When I had a good result he would come and say, "Look at this. This is fine. It is wonderful." But then when I had my liver scan, he came in without the chart. He said, "Oh, it's not ready yet." Now, I worked in a hospital so I know how fast they are. I asked, "How about the liver scan?" "It's all right," he said. "The liver is just slightly enlarged." I asked if I could see the report, but he said it wasn't back on the chart yet.

So the less he brought in the room, the worse I knew things were getting. Doctors do this a lot. I have seen it happen where I worked and I understand it, particularly when you have a personal relationship with your doctor. He is my friend as well as our family physician, and he would not come in the day after the operation. Nor did the surgeon come in. I was a blithering idiot. I was screaming and yelling because I firmly believe that the only thing worse than knowing you have cancer is thinking you have it and nobody telling you one way or the other. That is enough to drive you right up the wall. It really is.

I actually called his home and asked, "What was the result of the biopsy?" "I will be in tomorrow to tell you," he answered. It was, I think, probably the worst day of my entire life. Because I knew him well enough to know that if it had been good news he would have been there, and yet I didn't push him for the bad. And I certainly didn't want to push my husband, because I didn't know how much he knew. Maybe it is a defense mechanism to lie or avoid it all. If I had pushed my doctor, I think he would have told me on the phone, but I didn't. Because I wanted him there. I didn't want it over the phone.

I drove everybody on the staff crazy. I wouldn't eat. I would not do this or that. The nurses avoided me entirely. They didn't come into the room except to check the i.v. Nobody would talk to me. There was that feeling of isolation which continues throughout your hospitalization, particularly if you're young.

The nurses tend to identify with you. I have done it with young patients who have had bad diagnoses. Plus, I knew some of the girls, which made it more difficult for them. I know for a fact that two of them asked not to be assigned to me because they could not bring themselves to come in the room. Now I understand that. I saw myself in a girl who had breast cancer and eventually died. I think it is only natural when you're young and a young person has a diagnosis like this. The word "cancer" just brings such fear into the hearts of everyone. Treatment has changed since I was in nursing school. There is a great deal of hope with Hodgkin's disease, as with many other types of cancer. But to hear the word cancer, the family gives up on you, a lot of the people give up on themselves, and it is a shame because there are so many things that can be done now to extend life.

Marty: So what was it like when he finally told you?

Karen: He didn't. He came in the next day—late—and he asked, "Now what do you think you have?" and I said, "Hodgkin's disease." "You're right." So he got off pretty easy that way.

Marty: When he confirmed your diagnosis, did you feel relieved?

Karen: In a perverse way I was thrilled because now I *knew*. I wasn't crazy. This was not all in my head, and now we could treat it.

Because you don't know what's going on, you start to think that you are out of your mind. Short of a biopsy there is no specific test for Hodgkin's. And many of the symptoms are things you see with neurotic people—itching, not feeling good—nothing really specific. So you feel terrible saying you're not feeling good when you have no reason for not feeling good. When they told me, it was a relief. "Look at me! Look what I've got!" In a strange way I was proud. You don't want to have it, but "There is something wrong with me. I am sick." And in a way, you're happy.

I am not going to say I wasn't upset, but I am the type that when I'm upset I don't want anyone around me. This made it difficult for my husband, because he wanted to be with me and I wanted him away. I'm the sort that will go sit in the bathroom and talk to myself. After I have made up my mind how I feel about things, then you can all come and see me. Not until then. But I was so sure for so long, that it was not a big shock.

Marty: So you were relieved and a bit giddy. And proud, perhaps, that you could deal with it so well.

Karen: Right. I don't know, being a nurse, if I would have accepted a different disease as well. You don't know what you can cope with or not cope with. In Hodgkin's there are no pains involved. It's a pain in the neck to take the drugs and be sick from them for a two-week period. You are tired. You don't believe how tired you get. But there is not much pain.

I have seven brothers and sisters and we are all very close. One reason having Hodgkin's disease didn't bother me was that I was so glad it wasn't someone else I loved. I sat there for two hours one day and thought, "Who would I give this to, if it were in my power to give it to someone else?" The only person who came close was President Nixon—I just don't like the man—but that was only facetious. I honestly could not think of anyone. Why would you give someone else your illness? Even if you don't know them, like someone in Nairobi? What did he do? And that is why you have a great sense of peace. If you can say to yourself [that] it is within my power to give it to someone else and if you honestly wouldn't, how can you be mad or worry about it? I'd give the drugs to someone else if I could, but not the illness.

It was very hard for my husband. He is a practicing Roman Catholic, but in my way I think I am probably more religious than he is. He is older than I am and more rigid and goes to church and confessionals. He took this as a direct punishment from God, which is a terrible way to perceive illness. I don't take this as a punishment from God. People get sick and when people get sick, people die. There is a time and place for everything, so why blame it on God? That was hard for me to see him going through. A fear of God has been drummed into his head, not a love of God. That's why some extremely religious people find death so difficult.

Marty: You are talking about rote religion instead of its spirit.

Karen: Right. He's twelve years older than me, and we're from different generations as far as Catholicism is concerned. The Church and people in it have started to change, but he cannot. He's like my grandmother, who is eight-two and just had a mastectomy. She prayed to St. Anne every day of her life and now feels St. Anne let her down, so she'll never pray [to her] again. The idea that if I am good and I pray nothing bad will ever happen to me, doesn't make sense. It just doesn't. This eighty-two-year-old lady felt, "Why did God let this happen to me after all this time? I pray every day." Well yes, you pray every day. But that is not a life insurance policy. It is not "pay God six prayers a month and you won't get sick."

Marty: The drugs, I take it, are hard. How often do you take them?

Karen: The chemotherapy, two weeks on and two weeks off. And prednisone every other month. And they can cause more problems than my disease. Take the steroids. As a nurse, I knew that you can have euphoria or depression or both with them, but I had no idea of how severely those effects could be felt, particularly when you're taking large doses, as I am. During the first month on them I had euphoria. I was off the wall. If that's what being on a "high" is, it was fantastic. Everyone was wonderful. Nothing bothered me. The next time I was on it I was so depressed. Partly it came from the holidays. Holidays are the worst time when you have something like this, for your family as well. But I cannot begin to describe that state.

It's not depression where you simply sit down and cry. My husband could walk in the door and say "Hello. How are you?" and I'd take an ashtray and smash him over the head with it. It was a terrifying sensation to be rational enough to know that you are being irrational and still not be able to control it. People would look at me cross-eyed and it would bring me to tears. I'd know that I was crying for no reason and yet had to do it.

I think that illness is the great equalizer when it comes to doctors, nurses, or anyone who works in a hospital. You perpetually hand out pills, see side effects—vomiting, euphoria, depression— but you have no conception of what these drugs feel like inside. To you, vomiting is one time a day, when actually it can be thirty or forty times a day. Depression might mean that you don't feel like talking much, but it can also do terrible things to you. I really thought I was going out of my mind the second time I took prednisone. And I was not worried about dying as much as I was about prednisone and the holidays.

Marty: What was there about the holidays that got you?

Karen: A lot of things. When I got out of the hospital, my sister had a baby. I wanted to have children, which I will now never have, and I saw him for the first time. You don't resent other people, but you do resent their happiness in a way; that they are able to do and plan this, that, and the other without having to worry about jeopardizing their lives. Having a baby is only one example. There are a lot of places I'm not supposed to go and things I'm not supposed to do because of the dangers of infection. You're happy that others fare well, but there is a little bit of resentment. Envy is a better word than resentment.

There is also a feeling of closeness around the holidays. We are a very close family to begin with, and as sure as you are that you are going to be around for a while, there is some doubt about it. So you want to enjoy the family even more. But at that particular time, they were trying to isolate themselves from me. They did talk about happy things and good things, but if I started to talk about Hodgkin's disease—if one of the other family members would ask me something—my mother would be furious. I understand that it is difficult for her, but it is also difficult for me.

Or take my youngest brother. He is fourteen now and has always been the apple of everyone's eye. When he came to the hospital to see me, he didn't come into the room. I would say "Come in, Kenny," and he would say "No." He'd just stand in the doorway. I'd invite him in again and again I'd get a "No." I thought, well, I won't push him. Eventually he did walk in and said, "You don't look any different than you did before."

"But that is the point," I answered. "I am not any different than I was before."

I don't know what had been said to him at home, but he had a great fear, as though he was going to see me at death's door. He always used to let me come up and hug him and kiss him. But he won't let me do that anymore, and that hurts. I understand why. He doesn't want to get attached and then have something go wrong.

Marty: I suspect people also fear being contaminated by someone who has cancer.

Karen: How about that? Hodgkin's is not a contagious disease like chicken pox, but one theory is that you have antibodies that prevent you from getting it. Margaret's mother asked her, "Do you really think you should go and see Karen? You might get it."

People have asked me, "Is it contagious?" And then they pull away from you. With my youngest brother, it is very noticeable. He has transfered that hugging and kissing to another sister, and it hurts. It is sad to see people change toward you, and yet you do understand it. I don't know that I wouldn't be the same way in certain respects if the situation were reversed. But holidays are also the best of times, too, because you are there and it's wonderful. "Here I am alive and with my family. Isn't it great." So it's the best and the worst.

The idea that we won't have children upsets my husband and makes him unrealistic, which upsets me even more. I said something one day about going through menopause—which is what's happening under the drugs. He said, "Oh. But when that's over, we will have a baby." He knows it doesn't work that way, and it gets to me. His being totally unrealistic makes it doubly hard—his holding on to this hope of having a child when we never will. Adoption is out because of his age and my illness. I don't blame the agencies. I wouldn't give me one either.

He used to aggravate me, since he would not talk to me about my illness and seemed to bury his head in a hole. I know that a lot of nurses have morbid senses of humor. You say things, but you are just kidding around. It is a way of relieving tensions. But when I'd say little things, without thinking, like "over my dead body," he'd get all upset. "Don't say such things." "But you know," I'd tell him, "If you sit and worry about every little thing that you say, you are going to go out of your mind."

And while he didn't want to talk to me, he was also trying to be overly helpful. He said that he was going to drop out of school, even though he was finishing his Master's. That's when I said, "Over my dead body. After working this hard and this long, there is no way you're going to drop out of school. What is the point? It would be different if I were confined to bed and couldn't move, but I get around fine by myself. It's no big deal."

Then there were some funny situations. My husband is no tightwad, but when it comes to money we've invested in the stock market, God forbid you should touch that money. And I could not reconcile that here I was, in a way at death's door (and you can really get manipulative about this if you're not careful), that he knew it, yet would not take ten dollars out of the market to take me to dinner. Then recently he got sick. He had never been sick a day in his life and it made him appreciate what I must be feeling. That was the first time we really sat down and talked. This was only four months ago and it was then that he told me about this three-months-to-live business. So I said, "Here you are. You know I am not going to be alive more than a few weeks and you won't withdraw ten dollars to take me out. That makes it even worse." But he said, "The doctor told me not to change anything. I never took money out of the market before, so I wasn't going to take any out then." We both had a laugh over that one. I was incredulous. "I don't believe you." But my husband is very rigid in that sense. The doc told him not to change things, so that is what he did; not change anything. He was afraid that if he took one hundred dollars out of the market, I would know that I was going to die. I said, "I wouldn't have thought a thing except that you were trying to be nice and were taking me out to dinner once in a while."

He is a great deal bigger than I am; six-foot tall and weighing 210-215. He is a big man and once broke a little bone in my hand by grabbing me too tightly. So he was now afraid to come near me as far as sexual advances were concerned. Our doctor wrote, on a prescription blank, a great big heart with his initials and mine in it, and the prescription "Twice a day." Then it was all right. The doctor said it was all right. If someone didn't tell him it was all right he would worry and never come near me.

Marty: What do you do days?

Karen: I've started a little day school, a play school. I take in children during the day so that the mothers can play bridge or go shopping. And we have a wonderful time. We have a playroom in the house and it's really fun. People who visit think we have children. We have cribs and playpens. It is my way of compensating.

Somebody asked me, isn't that strange? Well, I don't see anything strange about it. If you can't have something, you make up your mind, "Okay. If I can't have it, I can play with other people's children. It helps them and it helps me."

Marty: Has having a fatal illness affected the way you live your life. Are there changes in regard to what you will do or not do?

Karen: Not at all. We wanted to buy a house for a long time, looked around, but couldn't find anything we could afford. Then we were hesitant, waiting to see how I'd do. But now we don't do anything differently than before. We don't go on round-the-world vacations. He still works as hard as he ever did. And I do the same things I used to except that I'm more careful.

Marty: You said that it helps you to talk things out but that it's hard to get people to listen. Just what do you like to talk out?

Karen: I find Hodgkin's disease a fascinating illness, particularly since I have it. I'm interested in the reactions of families to it and other forms of cancer. I think more should be done to help medical persons cope with their own feelings so that they can help the patient cope. And the patient can also help the family.

Marty: What would you want to see in a book about death and dying?

Karen: Just that it is not the worst thing in the world that can happen to you. Really and truly. I feel I would rather have this than be blind. I would rather have this than have no arms. Everything is relative to the individual. In your own mind you decide, "What is the worst thing in the world that could happen?" And I don't think that dying is it. To me, the worst thing in the world is throwing up every fifteen minutes for sixty hours. Now I have said that and people have laughed. But I mean it. I said that to my husband because I wanted to stop taking drugs and the doctors tried to discourage me. I was throwing up all the time. I've had patients say things like that to me, but I could not conceive, before, what they were talking about.

So I don't see death as being any terrible thing. We're born and we must die. It has to happen eventually. Certainly, I don't want to die tomorrow, but it's going to happen someday. I have also had very good experiences with patients, and I have seen very few of them who have fought death. Most people have died very beautifully. Death can be beautiful, in

a way, and I don't really fear being dead. I do not think it is all
that bad.

I feel sorry for the people left behind. I've always said that
it's much worse for them than for the dead. I won't know anything, so it's not a big deal. I just don't worry about it. Maybe
if I were closer to it I would be more upset, but I have always
felt this way. A lot of the things I would say in a book are
how to help families cope with relatives who have terminal
illness.

Marty: What would you tell them?

Karen: To think of themselves, not just the individual involved, because many of them have their own feelings. There
is nothing wrong with crying. You want someone to laugh *and*
cry with you, not just laugh. To know that someone cares about
you means they have to cry sometimes, and not just be around
in the good times.

I would ask the doctors to spend more time with the families.
Of necessity, their main concern is the patient. But they would
help the patient in the long run if they would spend more
time with the families.

Marty: What would they do during that time? Most doctors
are so busy that they don't spend much time anyplace.

Karen: That's true, too. You've seen it happen, I'm sure, that
when a person gets sick in a room with four people, as he
gets sicker he's moved to a double room. And then, when the
end is near, he goes to the end of the hall in a room by himself.
People are not stupid. They know that this is happening. I've
seen doctors abandon patients—you know, [they] put their
head in the door and [then] walk away. And the doctors
should be better able to cope with their own feelings.

Marty: But you would like them to guide the family more.

Karen: Tell them to be themselves and not try to change

things. This is the worst thing in the world that a person can do. At that particular time you don't need another change in your life. You're more in need of continuity. They should also tell families not to turn away. If you can't handle something, tell the ill person that you can't handle it. Don't change the subject or ignore it. Maybe you can't talk about it. I can understand that, but at least be honest enough with the patient to say, "I really cannot handle this." That is fine. You can accept that. But changing subjects or "I don't want to talk about it" really makes it difficult for you, because then you feel isolated.

Also, you don't stop caring for the other person just because you're sick, so they ought not to spare you their own bad news.

Marty: Who is "they"?

Karen: The outsider is always putting on this wonderful show. "Everything is going so well at work . . . at home . . . and the other place." Well, you don't want to be put out of touch with reality. You know that things cannot be all that wonderful everywhere. Sad things happen. Bad things happen all the time, and just because you're sick doesn't mean that people can only tell you happy or good things.

The reverse is also true sometimes. Some people, like my mother-in-law, are always morbid. She will always come in with, "Who died? Who died of cancer?" It starts to get on your nerves after a while. Be yourself. Talk about the things you always talked about.

Also, doctors should encourage more planning. I'm not talking about exact plans for your entire life, but you ought to make certain arrangements in the event that you were to die next month, or in two years, or whenever it happens to be. Practical things, like having a will, ought to be arranged.

Marty: Have you done that?

Karen: Yes. I've tried to talk to my husband about it, but again, that was at a very difficult time for him. I started making out a will. "Don't talk like that. I don't want to hear it." Whereas my mother, very unintentionally, the week I got out of the hospital, said, "Oh, by the way. I meant to tell you that you have to get your life insurance policy changed into your married name." I only felt funny when she said, "Oh my goodness!" She was absolutely horrified that she had mentioned a life insurance policy to me at this particular time. I thought it was hilarious and I told everybody about it. She, though, was mortified. But I made out a will. We didn't make out a joint will, because he wouldn't.

I've also gotten medical disability payments from my Social Security policy. I hope to return to work one of these days when I am off drugs and they decide it's safe for me.

Marty: Are there any periods of time when you get scared?

Karen: When I have a bad time with drugs. I am afraid to take them any longer, and I am afraid not to take them. There is always this thought that this might be the last time for that last malignant cell to be killed off. Yet I have had more than one side effect from the drugs. The last time, for absolutely no reason, all the tissue in my neck swelled up and I was scared to death. I was never so scared in my life, mainly because being unable to breathe is the most frightening sensation in the world. And I just said, afterward, "I won't take these drugs anymore because they are going to kill me. They will put on my tombstone, *Died of Side Effect of Drugs.* I don't want that." And when I read about personalities that have died, Frank McGee and Duke Ellington, they didn't die from cancer. They died of the side effects of their drugs. And I don't want to die an undignified death.

Marty: What is an undignified death?

Karen: Everybody running around and prolonging your life when there is no life. I would say if I were in a coma and they thought they ought to give me an i.v., I don't know that

I would want that. When it gets to the point where you're unresponsive, all these measures seem like a desecration of the human body. When I see these cardiac emergency teams running up to hospital rooms, it makes me almost physically ill—not so much when a young person is involved, but with older people. To me that is cruel—the heart massages and airways and injections and pacemakers seem done for practice, and not for saving someone's life.

Also, when I die, I don't want a wake. It's ridiculous and a waste. I just want to go wherever I'm going.

Marty: Have you talked that over with your husband?

Karen: Oh my, yes. That is in my will. He's not for that at all. I am a very practical person. I could not see the waste of money. I want to be cremated. I told him, "We have a fireplace in the house, that is the only way they are getting me out. Cremate me in the fireplace and let the ashes out. I do not see wasting money."

He said something about burying me with my rings; I have an engagement ring and a wedding band. I said, "God forbid you put that in my grave. That is the dumbest thing I ever heard. I am dead. I am certainly not getting any pleasure out of it. I would rather see it given to someone I love and have it continued on." To me, it is stupid, to put money in the ground, so to speak. He thinks I am just terrible. But I definitely want to be cremated. There is not enough room for the living. When the soul is gone, I'll be no different than a dead horse, or cow or dog.

Marty: What's your conception of what happens after death?

Karen: I believe there is a life hereafter. I don't know what it's like. In my own mind, hell is not fire and burning, but whatever you dislike the most, and that is where you have to stay. Heaven is a nice place. But a lot of my conceptions are a holdover.

For the moment, I am alive. And I would hope that the people I love and the people who know me could understand that what has happened is not the worst thing that can happen. You just want to be yourself and you don't want people changing themselves. If I could get people to fear cancer or death a little less, everyone would be much better off physically as well as mentally. But as a nation, we have always had a terrible fear of death. I don't think it's all that terrible.

9

An Ending
or a Beginning?

(Life After Death)

Death is not a puzzle to be solved any more than life is.
—Rev. Robert Neale

WHAT DOES DEATH feel like? Is there trauma? Does awareness
stop abruptly? And what of the possibility of life after death?

All religious dogma claims that there is continuity of life,
yet we tend to believe only what we directly apprehend. One
man claims he's talked with God. Another woman states she's
communicated with a dead relative at some seance. They have
their encounters and they believe. But if I've not undergone
a similar experience, I remain skeptical. To me, they might
be either misguided, or charlatans, or lunatics as well as tellers
of truth. Or simply people seeking comfort from an uncertain
existence in a bewildering universe.

There are, however, a myriad number of accounts by people who have approached or actually passed over the portals of clinical death. Although their stories are necessarily limited, these remain the best indicators we have as to what the end of life is about.

In 1871, Albert Heim, a Zurich geology professor and mountain climber, fell more than seventy feet while climbing.

"What I felt in five to ten seconds could not be described in ten times that length of time," he later wrote. "Mental activity became enormous, rising to a hundred-fold velocity."

At first he thought of practical things to do upon impact. Then his experiences became other-worldly.

"I saw my whole life take place in many images, as though on a stage at some distance from me. I saw myself as the chief character in the performance. Everything was transfigured as though by a heavenly light, and everything was beautiful without anxiety, and without pain. The memory of very tragic experiences I had had was clear but not saddening. I felt no conflict or strife; conflict had been transmuted into love. Elevated and harmonious thoughts dominated and united the individual images, and like magnificent music, a divine calm swept through my soul. I became ever more surrounded by a splendid blue heaven with delicate roseate-and-violet cloudlets. I swept into it painlessly and softly and saw that now I was falling freely through the air and that under me a snowfield lay waiting. Objective observations, thought, and subjective feelings were simultaneous."

Heim lost consciousness, but survived the fall with relatively minor injuries. He later collected anecdotes from others regarding near-fatal falls and in 1891 published his findings in the yearbook of the Swiss Alpine Club.

Ninety-five percent of those he interviewed reported experiences similar to his own. He concluded that people who actually do die from falls "have, in their last moments, reviewed their individual pasts in states of transfiguration. They have fondly thought of their loved ones. Elevated above corporeal pain, they were under the sway of noble and profound thoughts, heavenly music, and a feeling of peace and reconciliation."

Another account comes from a very sane and skeptical clinical psychologist I know who had a most uncanny experience twenty-five years ago. She was taken to an operating room for abdominal surgery and while under anesthesia had a "dream" that she had died.

She heard somebody say "She's gone," was cognizant of a doctor placing an oxygen tube down her nose, and listened to all the dialogue and commotion attending the surgeon's attempts to bring her back to life.

"Then I had this sensation of very slowly rising; feeling very light, as if I hadn't a body. I was moving up and up and up. There was a feeling of bigness around me, as if I were moving up and out; like a boat pulling out except that I didn't feel I was *in* anything.

"I also felt a sense of surprise, for in my mind I thought I had died and yet I felt so serene—not frightened at all. I was just happy and relaxed. I was still me, but I had no sense of sight or body. I just *was*.

"Then I thought of people who would be shocked and upset and grieved. I thought, 'If I can only communicate with them. If I can only reach them and tell them St. Paul was right, that there is no death, that I'm very happy and contented.' I wanted to convey to certain people my feelings of being comfortable and contented, of not having to struggle, of still being around."

My friend likened this episode to a very vivid hallucination until her next visit to the doctor after leaving the hospital.

"There were such unusual complications surrounding your operation that I want to go over them with you from beginning to end," he told her. He then described how she went into surgical shock, how both her heart and her breathing had ceased for several minutes, and how she had been clinically dead. He went on to recall the same conversations and activities that she heard during her "hallucination."

"I think of death now," my friend remarked, "as being

like a butterfly moving out of a cocoon; that perhaps we just emerge into a new life and live on a new channel in which we have no body for sensations but exist nonetheless."

These experiences of profound calmness, of sensing oneself in another dimension, of existing in a timeless and formless present moment, that Heim, his interviewees, and my therapist friend reported are similar to many other reputable accounts of people who have survived clinical death. They are also remarkably akin to reported religious states, whether brought on by meditation, pain, sensory deprivation, or psychedelic drugs.

Dr. Kübler-Ross has spoken with several dozen people who were also revived from clinical death. "They always experience the same thing," she noted in one interview. "There is a sensation of floating out a few feet above their bodies, along with an ability to observe and hear what is said in the goings-on about them. It is a most peaceful and most beautiful experience that they describe. They want to tell everybody working on them, 'Relax. Take it easy. It's okay.' But the more they try, the more frantic the people trying to save them become.

"Once they have experienced death, they are not ever afraid to die."

Such contacts with the dying as these have changed Kübler-Ross from a "wishy-washy Protestant with no belief in a life after death to a person who does now believe in an afterlife, but in a non churchy way."

If most of our scientific thinkers insist that no one has ever come back to life after dying, if they would scoff at reports like those of Bishop James Pike, who reported being in contact with his dead son,* if they would attempt to prove that my friend's death in the operating room was not real, what of it?

"If your friend was revived," I would be told, "she wasn't really dead to begin with." Does this prove the scientists' point? Or is it merely a word game that a skeptic engages in to prove his own prejudgment—that the dead cannot go on living?

---

*James Pike. *The Other Side.* London: W. H. Allen & Co., 1969.

I prefer to think of such tales as roadmaps which bring us to the very edge of a vast and unchartered territory. It is a land we shall eventually know only when we ourselves make that ultimate journey. But the indicators are that it is not as terrifying as we might have feared.

From time immemorial, humans have believed in a world of spirits. Throughout thousands of differing religious sects, death is invariably regarded as a crisis through which the deceased enters a new status. From preliterate religions to Judaeo-Christian concepts, from Islam to Eastern religious thought, this idea is clear: While the body may disintegrate, the entity or power that gave it life cannot vanish. It may be transformed, but not eliminated. Death is viewed as one phase in the career of some living force that dwells in a body for some time but neither begins nor ends with it.

Primitive religions have not usually postulated a hierarchy of rewards and punishments in the world of the dead. All major contemporary religions do, just as they equate one's worldly being to one's fate after death. Allah ensures a true Moslem believer a happy place in the hereafter. A Buddhist can achieve Nirvana through a long succession of reincarnations, provided that his actions (*karma*) during these lives justify it. Hinduism relates *moksa* (salvation) to *dharma* (civic and religious piety). Both Christian and Jew are constantly observed by God and will be rewarded or punished in the afterlife depending upon their thought and conduct.

Contemporary Eastern and Western religions differ in emphasis, not in essentials. In the East, contemplation and mysticism are emphasized as the way to achieve salvation. In the West, the predominant quest is made through hard work and righteous public efforts. The Easterner sees the eventual outcome as an undifferentiated merging with the oneness of the universe. Western man envisions a continuity of his personal self, transported into heaven, where he can contemplate not only a separate god but other well-defined entities.

If each of us could be truly convinced that there was a continuation of consciousness beyond our mortal life, death might lose much of its terror. The scariest thing for most of us is the idea of THE END; that we are here one moment and gone the next, like a light switch that is abruptly turned on and off. Those who are convinced that awareness does not cease with death face dying with particular calmness and detachment. That was true of Bill in our earlier interview. It is also apparent in Sister Mary Catherine, a fifty-three-year-old librarian at a school run by her order.

She answered an advertisement I put in a local newspaper asking for dying people to tell their stories. She arrived at my office dressed in her habit. Slim, of medium height, with clear eyes, pale skin, and a pleasant smile, she epitomized unselfconsciousness, unstudied compassion, and tranquillity.

Radiating a calmness that transcends the printed transcript, her delicacy and shyness reinforced a feeling of unpretentious, authentic spirituality. She never feared death. Her belief in something afterwards was so certain that she was prepared to cease her treatments and die a natural death. And yet, as she said, her focus is on "life and what I can do now."

Seeing her, I was reminded of the words of a Yale University chaplain who talked of an afterlife. "That doesn't mean one has to hurry to get there," he said, "or that it's superior. I think of it as an extension and progression of where we are now. We all get there when we get there. Our present is just as important, for it's one continuous flow."

* * *

Mary Catherine: In the summer of '72 I had a radical mastectomy. In reading about it I understood that if you don't have any recurrence within five years, your chances are pretty good. But after one and a half years I had a recurrence and had treatment in four different areas. So right now I am getting chemotherapy injections and treatments. The doctors did tell me that the treatment may make me very uncomfortable or it may cure me. They don't know. It is not very predictable.

Marty: How did it all come about? When did you first become aware of having cancer.

Mary Catherine: Well, I had a very heavy cold and I could not get rid of it. In June I went to the doctor to ask him for something. He examined me and discovered a small lump. He is a general practitioner, so he immediately called to have me see a surgeon. When that doctor examined me he said, "Sister, we can never tell exactly what is what, but from looking at it I think you need a mastectomy operation."

When they operated, they sent for a biopsy immediately and did find it was malignant. Then, when the final reports came in, they found that I had cancer in several of the lymph nodes under the arm.

Marty: How did you feel when you first found out about it? What was your first reaction?

Mary Catherine: Like everyone else, you imagine the worst. I think most people jump to that conclusion and get very excited. But I think I am in a better position than some people. I have responsibilities within my own living circumstances. But I don't have responsibilities like a husband and children.

I was in the hospital this summer and the lady in the same room with me came in because of a lump on her breast. She had a husband and a daughter. Before she left we became quite good friends, because I was with her and helped to ease her fear of the operation. When she came back from the operation she had no malignancy or anything, only a cyst. But she said it was the best thing in the world for her that I was in the hospital.

Marty: How did you help her?

Mary Catherine: I spoke to her about my feelings. I was sympathetic with her, but on one occasion I was not too sympathetic. I explained to her that an operation such as a mastectomy is not the end of everything, and I told her that I was back on full duty. I didn't tell, though, that I had all the treatments previous to this because I had a feeling that as things come, you learn to accept them. I don't think you can handle everything at once.

Marty: I would like to know more about what you did for her that she found helpful. What can you do for people that is helpful, rather than just useless chatter?

Mary Catherine: First of all, I did tell her the effects of the operation. I told her that it took me a little while to gain back my strength. First I told her my reactions. Then I told her that the doctor told me to exercise once a day. But a nurse sister living in the convent told me to exercise more.

Marty: You said that at one time you were not sympathetic with her at all. What was that about?

Mary Catherine: She was ready to give in, and it was the end of everything for her. She would not be good for anything anymore. Then I really was not sympathetic. I said, "You have to be positive. Your chances are good that even if you do have a radical mastectomy it is not going to be the end of everything. There are many people who have such operations and pull through. You will have to take it easy for a little while, but it is not everything."

Marty: Going back to your experience, when they made the diagnosis, were there moments of terror or anguish or great fear?

Mary Catherine: I am a Catholic, naturally, and I do really believe in life after death. That is one of my strong convictions. I had a fairly full life, and as I look back, I don't really have any big weaknesses or regrets. Maybe I should fear dying. I am not looking forward to it. I would not hasten it. But I am not really afraid of dying, because I feel there is more to present life than just material things. I think there has to be something after. I have to believe that or I would not have given up my life for service.

Marty: I asked you that question because Elisabeth Kübler-Ross has interviewed hundreds of dying people in hospitals, and her evaluation was that religious people do not fare any better than agnostic or irreligious people in terms of being prepared to accept their terminality. This is interesting to me. I would have thought that a person steeped in religious tradition would die more easily than those who weren't. I assume she was describing those in formal religions as opposed to those who feel it in their souls.

Mary Catherine: Maybe I am different, but I have never really been afraid of death, even when I knew I had the mastectomy. When I went to the operating room, the doctor didn't know what kind of operation it would turn out to be. And when I came down and realized what it was, I was not really frightened. Then, almost a year ago, when I discovered this other lump, I realized that my chances were not too good of surviving much longer. And I usually have pain. I have it in quite a few places. I have it in my back, sometimes in my arms, my legs, but I don't have to take heavy medication and there is no fear.

The things we have that are physical, when you get down to it, are so unimportant. As for people who just believe in this life, I think that death, for them, must be much harder.

If you are really sick in bed, I think some people don't really care if they are dying. I think they welcome it. I know when I felt very sick—sometimes, if I had died a minute later, I don't think I would have gotten upset.

I have been very fortunate. I have met with doctors who are very skillful. And the sisters I live with are all very nice people. I am in school all day. I work at the library, but my duties have been lessened quite a bit and I don't have the pressure of a heavy job .

Marty: You talk about being comforted by life after death. What do you think occurs afterward?

Mary Catherine: I really don't have any clear idea, but I have always felt that there is such a thing as eternity. We are on earth for a limited time; after death there has to be something far superior to what we have now. Because physically, there are a great many good things and a great many hard things, a great many evil things. And my idea of heaven, really, is being related to God in a spiritual way. It is not a physical thing. All through my life I feel as if I have been fairly close to God, and I think that when I reach heaven (I hope I will reach heaven) it will be God's home that I will be part of. And I don't think it is limited to one personification. I think it encompasses everyone. But I am sure I have a special spot.

Marty: How do you plan to deal with the future? Any special plans? Or do you think you will just keep working?

Mary Catherine: I think most about life and what I can do now. But I am at the point where I want to speak to one of the doctors that I have been going to. I am considering not continuing the treatments. I really don't see why I should. I think that my pain is less than it was. I would have really severe pains before. Now they are bearable, and I just wonder if it's worth going to get these treatments. Because when I get them I am knocked out for a few days. And I just wonder. I spoke to a clergyman . . .

Marty: You would just rather go along with the natural disease?

Mary Catherine: I don't know. That's what I'm thinking. I

know I saw my mother dying and they did everything they could to keep her alive. And I don't believe in that, because she had a clear mind up to an hour before she died. I don't think you should hasten anyone's death, but I do think that, as you say, a natural death is all right. I did speak to a clergyman, and he said I have a right to decide, if I wish. So if I decide to stop the treatments, I can. Without any responsibilities. I think if I had a family, I would continue.

Then, if I could meet up with the right person, I would like to see if I have anything that is worth donating; any organs . . . I have good eyes, my heart is good so far, my kidneys are good, and so forth. If I had any organs that could be used, I would like to donate them and after that, truthfully, I don't care.

Marty: What would you look for in a book on death? What kind of focus would you want it to have?

Mary Catherine: I would like to see some kind of encouragement given to people who don't believe in anything beyond this life. That is what I think exists. It's not a good comparison, and it may be farfetched but, for example, what happened way back in history affects us even today. I think there has to be a continuation of life in some way. And for me, a continuation of life is being united with God.

SOME LAST WORDS

Now comes the mystery.

—Henry Ward Beecher

Woe's me. Methinks I'm turning into a God.

—the Emperor Vaspasian

The mountain is passed; now we shall get on better.

—Frederick the Great

Why fear death? It is the most beautiful adventure in life.
—Charles Frohman

Let us go over the river, and sit in the shade of the trees.
—T. J. (Stonewall) Jackson

This is the last of earth! I am content.
—John Quincy Adams

Now I am about to take my last voyage, a great leap in the dark.
—Thomas Hobbes

Even going my journey, they have greased my boots already.
—Samuel Garth (after receiving Extreme Unction)

Clasp my hand, dear friend, I am dying.
—Vittorio Afieri

10

Overcoming the Fear of Death

The fear of death is more to be dreaded than death.
—Publius Syrus

STRONG EMOTIONS REVERBERATE—what we feel influences those about us. A tranquil person has a soothing effect upon others he comes in contact with. The anxious man transmits his jitters.

If you are comfortable with the idea of dying, you will be a source of comfort to those who need your help. It is therefore imperative that we consider the fears that death evokes within us. Fear is always indescribable. Articulating just what it is that we dread contributes to diminishing its effects. Breaking down the terror to its component parts also makes constructive countermeasures obvious.

Eventually, of course, nearly everyone overcomes the fear of death and enters a state of accepting it. The question, then, is how soon this fear can be dispelled. The answer depends upon how rapidly one understands the scarifying subelements and how ready one is to come to terms with each.

Let us consider the fear of contamination. Many people have not progressed beyond the concepts held by ancient Hebrews, who regarded the body of a dead person as something unclean and not to be touched. We can handle dead pets or sides of beef, but are peculiarly loath to make physical contact with dead or even dying people.

When I arrived at my parents' house during my father's final hours, I was struck by the physical positioning of everyone in the living room. My dad's bed was the couch, which lay against one wall. In the farthest corners of the room sat his sister, his wife, and his daughter. I welcomed the opportunity to pull a chair over to his bedside and hold his hand for the next several hours, to lessen the isolation I felt he experienced. We could in this way caress one another as he gradually weakened and died, for I recognized the fear of contamination as primitive superstition.

A fear such as this has its roots in our childhood and stems from parental injunctions given, oddly enough, to ensure our survival. The tragedy is that such messages also produce a fear of the unknown and unfamiliar, an anticipatory fear that has been drummed into most of us in the course of our upbringing.

Countless parents have taught countless children not to do this, that, or some other thing "or you might get killed." Some of these prohibitions are ludicrous, like "don't drink from someone else's glass or you can catch germs and die." Others, such as "don't talk to strangers, they could be kidnappers or murderers," represent gross exaggerations. We are cautioned against playing with matches, crossing a crowded street, or going out in the wintertime without overshoes. All these events and more could lead to our destruction. Caution in living is the watchword. The risk of not heeding these restrictions is a slap on the backside or some other punishment. And these punishments are administered in the name of helping us avoid an even larger punishment—death!

> He who does not fear death, cares naught for threats.
> —Pierre Corneille

"Forewarned is forearmed," an old maxim reads. Given the magnitude of these early lessons, however, we might equally say that forewarning leads to foreboding.

One does not talk readily with either friends or strangers about the fear of death and its implications for life. Nor are we provided with decent psychological guidelines.

Although psychiatrists have delved into most areas of human stress, they have largely avoided death as a subject of inquiry. Part of this avoidance is because death has been such an affront to the dignity of the physicians or psychiatrists who struggle tooth and nail to keep their patients alive forever. When they don't, they feel guilty or inadequate. A medical practitioner who loses a patient does not feel as competent as his colleague who has kept someone in a coma alive for an extra three months and proved his greater medical skills. And a therapist whose client commits suicide feels too personally responsible to open up the case fully for public exploration. This unwillingness to enter into meaningful dialogues on death—to substitute a conspiracy of silence for shared stories and common experiences—only contributes to a festering anxiety.

> No man can be living forever, and we must be satisfied.
> —J .M. Synge

The secular beliefs that define our society also cause death to be a tabooed subject. Youth, health, and affluence are held in such high regard that aging and death are seen as anti-American. They are feared and not discussed because they threaten those values we most cherish.

How does one overcome this fear of the unmentionable, the unknown, and the unfamiliar? By being open to thoughts of death, by being willing to discuss one's feelings, and by spending time with people who are dying.

I've been convinced, on countless occasions in the past, that I would die in particular ways. As a child I was sure that a werewolf would devour me. As an adolescent I would perish in a roller-coaster crash. Later I was certain that I'd die in a gang fight. In my twenties I'd be done in by prostatic cancer, since both my grandfathers had had it. At thirty, a sudden siege of chest pain convinced me that a heart attack would seal my doom.

> He who fears death dies every time he thinks of it.
>
> —Stanislaus Lesycynski

I am glad now that I allowed myself these thoughts, that I did not try to push them out of my mind. Having made it to forty, I'm much less concerned about death. If I occasionally think of dying in a particular way, I recall that I've fantasized ending up in a hundred different manners—from dozens of strange and common diseases, to mangling accidents in cars and planes, to being victimized by some mad intruder. Memories of these earlier scares help me expose my current apprehension as mere imagination. The feeling that remains is "it will happen when it will happen."

Spending time with my father was also quite helpful. I knew he had to die. He knew he had to die. We had always enjoyed and loved each other, and so we saw each other frequently during his final months. I came to value the all-rightness of the dying process, the dignity in it, and the ability one has to deal with pain. His slow fading away, his good days and his bad ones, made me see that a man or woman can live richly up until the last breath is taken; that a dying person can truly savor and enjoy life to its very end.

> Are you afraid you won't know how to die? Don't worry. Nature will take care of it for you.
> —Marco Vassi

The fear of living an incomplete life must also be overcome. Death is a threat largely because it eliminates the opportunity to achieve goals important to self-esteem or because it deprives one of a chance to have longed-for experiences.

At age thirty-five, I had a vivid premonition that I would die in two years. Believing that, I made sure that my life was as complete as I could make it on a day-to-day basis. Trips I wanted to take, people I wanted to see, words I wanted to write, involvements I wanted to have were carried out to the limits of my capabilities. In doing all I wished to do, I felt that I had pretty well encompassed everything by the time my thirty-seventh birthday had arrived. From then on, whatever other enjoyable experiences I might have—be it lying in the sun, partaking of a feast, making a "discovery," indulging my eroticism, enjoying the company of a friend—would be essentially replays. The characters and events might change, but the basic scenarios and responses would not.

At that point I could begin to glimpse an exciting element in death. It was the same excitement I had earlier learned to recognize and welcome which preceded any venture into something new, different, and challenging. And death, at that time in my life, would remain the only totally new and novel ex-

perience I could look forward to. This turnabout from anxiety
to excitement fit in perfectly with a previous conceptualiza-
tion that what we label anxiety is simply a charged energy
state to which we assign a negative label.

To avoid the fear of living an incomplete life requires that
we live as fully as possible today, that we embark upon and
complete those tasks we feel to be significant.

The protagonist of the Japanese film classic *Ikiru* was a clerk
whose life was totally devoid of meaning. After learning that
he had stomach cancer, he became involved in a struggle to
build a playground for some children. That was his fulfillment, which enabled him to die with dignity and satisfaction.

Fulfillment often represents the culmination of some life-
long desire. The Indian who's able to travel to Benares to
die is fulfilled, as is the housewife from Topeka who has
always wanted to visit Maui, or the woman of thirty-six who
would feel satisfied if she would only know love and marriage.
Or experience orgasm. Or live to see her grandchildren. Some
of these things we can complete by dint of our own efforts,
others we cannot. Still, knowing one has tried one's utmost
provides significant comfort.

Death fear, like anxiety in general, is invariably related to
a situation that has not yet arisen. It is an anticipatory emotion, not an actual one. Although thoughts and meditation
can make death more acceptable, so can the nonthinking position, particularly if it is coupled with attention to the actual-
ities of present-day living. Death always occurs in a future
tomorrow. Live in the present and you are, in fact, living in
time immemorial.

If much of life is a quest for individuality, the awareness of
death impels us to seek union. We aspire toward a connection
larger than life, for some joining with the cosmos. This union
has many names. "Immortality," "afterlife," "ego transcendence" are just some of them. Those who've experienced it,
like Sister Mary Catherine, are not afraid to die. Unfortu-
nately, the secularization of American religion has failed to

provide such comfort for most others. Thus we come to our most significant fear, the fear of a final ending.

Not having had any formal religious training myself, I had always presumed that those who attended church services regularly did so in the hope of attaining everlasting life or some guarantee that their essences would continue after their bodies fell by the wayside. I was totally unprepared when a high official in the Episcopal Church challenged my assumption.

"People don't come to church to combat their terror of death," he said. "Most of them are here simply because they're lonely and want to be around other people."

The twentieth century's new religion, Science, further undermined traditional notions of immortality by casting doubt upon the allegories concerning Creation. This caused people to abandon the idea of a personal immortality and afterlife and to substitute, instead, a compensating notion of social immortality. We might not live on, but we could count on living through our children. But science later created the ultimate doomsday weapon, the constant threat of nuclear holocaust and global annihilation destroying any solace we might have received from social-immortality concepts.

> All our knowledge merely helps us to die a more painful death than the animals that know nothing.
> —Maurice Maeterlinck

In this vacuum, many have come to discover states of ego-transcendence through the use of psychedelic drugs. A nation of experience seekers, we have continuously explored, used, and abused various chemical agents that alter both our physical and mental states. Some of these agents—particularly mescaline, lysergic acid, and psilocybin—along with other psychedelic drugs, have the effect of momentarily releasing the ingestor from his ego. That is to say, the user loses total awareness of his body, personality, identifications, and habitual reaction patterns and exists for a limited period of time in a state that's been described as pure consciousness. Carlos Casteneda, in his books about Don Juan, has reported how an old Indian *brujo* employs these drugs to get in touch with another world, his separate reality.

Whether one accepts such accounts as factual or not, there is no doubt that these chemicals have helped take the sting out of death for many people. "Experiential Transcendence is a model for and a path toward an altered relationship to time and death," state Yale psychiatrist Robert Jay Lifton and his collaborator, Eric Olson, in their book *Living and Dying,* when they discuss the influence of these agents. I and many others would agree with them. The National Institute for Mental Health has been using LSD effectively with terminal cancer patients for some time, finding that whatever that mystical, awesome experience is that a person has on the drug—entering an Unknown that makes life more tolerable, experiencing yourself as part and parcel of creation, witnessing the eternal present—can produce an easier appreciation and acceptance of the life-death cycle. Though it is a contradiction to think of preparing oneself for what is unknown, it seems to be a fact that those who "unprepare" themselves best are people who have had some transcendent experience.

> The long habit of living indisposeth us for dying.
> —Thomas Browne

Our faith in science and technology, our well-equipped hospitals, and our loathing of death have given rise to the false hope that, given the proper resources and research, all of mans' life-threatening ills can be done away with. Such illusions mask our basic anxiety but do nothing to dispel it.

We have been seduced into believing that cancer will and should be overcome if only we donate enough money to the cancer society. Heart disease might vanish if we give generously to the heart foundation. Tuberculosis can be conquered if we only keep sending in our dimes. Automobiles can and ought to be made safe if the government and General Motors develop and demand new safety features. Wars can be ended, given a proper study of history, or a better world government. Pollution can be halted, given scientific industry. Famine can be eliminated if we farm the sea.

Semen and freshly expired corpses are being frozen in attempts to preserve them until that never-never day when technology conquers nature, when death can be perpetually avoided and life, like a summer vacation, can go on forever.

But death, though postponable, is inevitable. Heart disease, accidents, cancer are just nature's way of kissing us good-bye. If we discovered cures for all these ills, she would invent other ways of keeping us in the never-ending circle of transformations.

There is no cure for birth or death save to enjoy the interlude.

—George Santayana

11

Planning Ahead: Wills, Finances, and Funerals

THE OWNER OF a prosperous luncheonette dies. Although without much liquid capital, he had been bringing home eight hundred dollars a week to support a family of five. Upon his sudden death, the family finds itself without any immediate income. His life-insurance policy is barely sufficient to ensure financial security for more than a year or two after his debts are paid off. In addition, the government insists on a sizable inheritance tax based upon the receipts of his restaurant. In-

---

The author is especially grateful to Jack Rabin, whose legal advice helped shape this chapter.

stead of his wife's being able to run the establishment herself, she must sell it at a decided loss in order to meet this unexpected bill.

An old woman dies, leaving her prized jewelery in a safe-deposit vault. She had meant to give them as gifts to her granddaughter. The girl, neither knowing where the vault was nor having had advance permission to open the box, loses the intended legacy. The contents of the vault are instead opened under state inspection, taxed, and divided among other inheritors.

Two recent widows are left moderate estates of comparable value. The one whose husband left a will pays eight thousand dollars in taxes. The other pays thirty thousand dollars.

These demoralizing events and many more could have been avoided if plans had been made ahead of time. That plans are often neglected has to do with our own refusal to accept the likelihood of death, and with primitive beliefs that planning for someone's demise might magically hasten it.

In her book, *Widow,* Lynn Caine make a strong case for what she has named Contingency-Day Planning. Once a year, she suggests, perhaps on an anniversary, a couple ought to overcome their taboos and review all financial matters that are germaine, since there is no doubt that one day death will occur. What does one review on Contingency Day? For starters, one ought to know where all bank accounts, real estate deeds, wills, pensions, insurance policies, stocks, cash, mortgages, debt records, payment books, receipts, old tax returns, and safe-deposit-vault keys are kept.

Secondly, one ought to be aware of measures to be taken, both before death and afterward, so as to minimize stress. Death can cause severe financial difficulties for the survivors. Wives are called upon to handle monetary transactions that they are totally unfamiliar with. Parents, children, or spouses who relied upon the wage earner may have to find other sources of income. The assets and funds of the deceased are immediately frozen until a will is probated (proven to be authentic) or intestacy matters (the legal provisions that must be adhered to when one dies without a will) are settled, yet living expenses must come from somewhere. If you are part of the immediate family of a terminally ill adult, you most definitely ought to ask them what provision, if any, they've made or wish to make for the future. When every nickel counts, one ought to make concrete plans and familiarize oneself with outside resources.

WILLS

There is no step more important than having a properly drawn will, and yet only 24 percent of Americans execute them. Each state makes very specific provision for the settling of an estate when someone dies intestate (without a will). These provisions frequently work to the great disadvantage of the survivors. A reasonably executed will can reduce both the expense and the aggravation that result from having court-appointed administrators, can save thousands of dollars in taxes, and can apportion assets according to the wishes of the dying, under the guidance of someone they trust.

Wills are not simply things for the wealthy. If a millionaire dies without one (and many have) and the government takes out a quarter of a million dollars in taxes, his survivors still have three-quarters of a million dollars left to live on. Assuming that there are two or more children involved, his wife is entitled to a third of the remaining estate, or another $250,000. But if a family man with a net worth of thirty thousand dollars dies, and his wife can only utilize ten thousand dollars of that amount, there may be problems.

When one dies, someone must be legally responsible for settling the estate, paying debts and taxes and dividing up assets among the heirs. With a will, one names their own executor to do this. The executor is usually the spouse, but can be anyone you feel confident with. Without a will, the surrogate court appoints an administrator, who may be the spouse or may be some clubhouse lawyer who is owed a political favor.

The laws of intestacy in New York, like those of most other states, provide that if the surviving parent has two or more children, one-third of the estate is left to the spouse and two-thirds to the children. The administrator is suposed to see that the children's funds are held for them until they come of age. Suppose that a man leaves thirty thousand dollars and has no will. When his wife needs extra funds for her four- and five-year-olds, having spent the ten thousand dollars she was left over a period of fifteen months, she must petition the court for this money and show cause why she should be allowed to withdraw it. This is true even if the court appointed her to be the guardian. Petitions mean legal fees, and with such a small inheritance, one cannot readily afford them. Also, a yearly report must be filed by the administrator—again more hassles and more fees. Leaving your entire estate to your spouse or naming an executor in a will avoids these complications.

Tax savings, under a will, can also be considerable on any estate valued at $120,000 and up. Nor is that figure as out of the ordinary as it might sound. The average middle- management executive, businessman, or professional is often worth that much or more.

A couple may have purchased a house ten years ago which has by now doubled in value. Their equity in it might be assessed realistically at $25,000. The furnishings inside are probably worth an additional $15,000. Add a $50,000 group life-insurance policy, eighteen to twenty thousand dollars a year in salary, a car, some stocks, and bank accounts, and the figure readily climbs above $120,000.

Under federal tax law, there is an exemption for that part of the estate left the spouse, up to one-half the total value. There is another statutory tax exemption of sixty-thousand dollars upon any estate. That means that if a will is drawn leaving all of the estate to the wife, there are no taxes to pay (sixty thousand dollars is exempt, and the second sixty thousand dollars is exempt by statute). As the value of an estate mounts, so do the potential tax savings. If the deceased was married, had a couple of children, and had a net worth of two hundred thousand dollars, the tax bill would ordinarily be $29,800. By drawing a will and taking advantage of the marital deduction (where the wife is left half the estate instead of two-thirds) taxes are reduced to $7,300, a savings of more than $22,000.

Naming a financially responsible executor enables you to provide the best protection for the living. Suppose both parents perish in an automobile accident. Brother Joe loves your kids and would gladly take them in, but he has a long record of financial mismanagement and business failures. In a will, one can appoint him as the kids' guardian and someone else to manage the funds. Or perhaps one's spouse is a poor money handler. Again, a trusted friend or a trust fund can fill this gap.

Wills can be properly drawn quite inexpensively. A simple one will be executed by most attorneys for seventy-five dollars to one hundred dollars. More complex, if costly, estate planning is also available through lawyers who specialize in this. If, for instance, a man has a successful business that brings in one hundred thousand dollars a year, the government may value the estate (including his business) at several hundred thousand dollars. The inheritance tax might be $40,000 or more. If there is not enough cash on hand, a forced sale of the business for less than its true value might be necessary in order to pay the tax bill. A decent estate planner would have recommended cheap term insurance to cover this possibility.

A competent attorney or estate planner could also advise on ways to save inheritance taxes that are not dependent on wills. Many individuals choose to divest themselves of their estates before they die. One way of doing this is through intervivos trusts, in which all money is put into trust funds for others. Income from these trusts can then be passed on to survivors without the principal being heavily taxed because of death. Still another means of divestiture concerns gifts. One can give three thousand dollars apiece, tax free, to as many individuals as one wishes in every calendar year.

INSURANCE

Although most people have some life insurance, 20 percent of Americans do not. And policies written years ago have frequently been found wanting due to increased family size and the ravages of inflation.

Most states require that life insurance policies have two-year incontestability clauses, and many companies, as a sales pitch, offer a one-year incontestability clause. These clauses mean that if the decedent lived for either one or two years after securing a policy, the company must pay benefits *even if the insured lied about his or her health when obtaining the policy.* Incontestability laws were originally passed to prevent companies from unfairly refusing to pay benefits or hassling survivors by claiming that all was not proper when the contract was executed.

These laws can be used to a sick person's advantage, for there is nothing amiss for anyone who has a premonition that something might be physically wrong with them to go apply for an inexpensive *term* life-insurance policy (term insurance provides death benefits only, not retirement funds) prior to a thorough checkup. Costly policies might require some standard but often perfunctory medical examination. Less costly ones often waive them.

SOCIAL SECURITY

An important source of income is potentially available to anyone disabled by a chronic or fatal illness prior to death. Social Security also pays a death benefit of $255 to the insured's family to cover funeral expenses.

The greatest dividends are found in survivors' benefits, which are paid to widows, widowers, or dependent children. This can come to as much as $720 a month for a widow with two dependent children, and should never be overlooked. So, Contingency-Day Planning must include a knowledge of where such documents as marriage licenses, birth certificates, and Social Security numbers are kept. You can write to or telephone your local Social Security office for a full listing of benefits.

VETERANS' ADMINISTRATION

A veteran's family is entitled to four hundred dollars in funeral expenses if one is buried privately, or free burial in any national cemetery. In addition, there are dependency and indemnity compensations available to dependents for any service-related death, even if these deaths occur fifteen or more years later.

Another benefit accrues to children between the ages of eighteen and twenty-six whose parent died or was disabled by service-related injuries, for they are eligible for scholarship and educational stipends. If you supply your local V.A. office with proof of service (the Selective Service number will do), they can give you further details and make the necessary arrangements.

PENSIONS

Although only 2 to 3 percent of private pension plans make provisions for widows, those programs offered to civil service workers do better. In any event, one ought to check them out as part of Contingency-Day Planning. If death has already occurred, a phone call to the deceased's office or the local civil service union in your city or state would be worthwhile.

Survivors of servicemen who die on military duty are entitled to six months of salary as a death benefit. Railroad workers' families are also eligible for special pension benefits. Potential survivors of employees on other federal jobs would do well to investigate if they, too, are entitled to benefits.

BANK LOANS

Personal loans often include term life-insurance payments, so that if a death occurs, the loan is paid off (similar provisions are sometimes made in home mortgages) and the borrowed money remains available for use. Again, if one suspects trouble, a loan of this type can provide a few extra and much-needed dollars for one's family.

FUNERALS

Animals do not have a problem concerning the disposition of the dead. They simply return to the forms from which they came. Insects, birds, and other beasts fall and, like trees or leaves, reenter the soil. Their remains are processed through the appetites of living beings that feed on them—by other beasts, fungi, or bacteria—and are dissolved by the falling rain and snow. This incredibly rich and complex function of decomposition represents nature's ultimate recycling process, validating the Biblical admonition that "from dust thou art and unto dust shalt thou return."

Mankind has not been so fortunate. For one thing, we are not at all certain that returning to dust is best for us. If pharaohs could be preserved forever in their great pyramids and Lenin hermetically sealed in the Kremlin, every American, in this great democracy, could rest embalmed and untouched in his copper-lined concrete casket at Forest Lawn.

Earlier traditions, from ancient times onward (including nineteenth-century America and Europe), had at least two advantages over contemporary domestic practices. Families frequently buried their own dead, hiring undertakers only when friends or relatives were unable or unwilling to undertake the task themselves. Also, they were more in touch with the symbolic significance surrounding funerals.

Throughout recorded time, funerals have served multiple ritualistic purposes above and beyond the necessary disposal of the body. One of these has been to safeguard the living against spirits.

Usually we die with our eyes open, but traditionally have them sealed in order to prevent us from staring at the living, from giving them the evil eye. Rituals of taking the corpse to the grave site by roundabout routes were meant to confuse ghosts and prevent their return, as was the custom of strewing thorns along the processional path. Also, destroying the possessions of the dead would make them unwelcome in their old homes. And the tombstone not only served a function as a monument but as a heavy weight that would keep the dead securely in the ground.

There are also rites-of-passage aspects to funerals; those measures which are taken to give the spirit assistance in finding rest and peace. Ancient Egyptians, Norsemen, and innumerable other peoples buried their dead with tools and ships and jewels for use in the afterlife. A fussy God would certainly be more inclined to accept a well groomed, manicured, washed, dressed, and anointed corpse than he would one hastily put in a sack. Magical sounds and words formed prayers, uttered by mourners to invoke the Lord's good grace, and the tears and cries of professional wailers were designed to move the Divine Soul to sympathy and compassion. The holy men of every culture—the shamans, priests, pastors, monks, and rabbis—are invariably utilized to intercede with the Creator to aid the deceased's transition to a more beatific existence. Cremation, in the East, not only disposes of the body but cleanses and frees the soul so that it might more readily pass on to its next state.

A third aspect of the funeral stresses the resolution of grief. Our emotions are altered in one of two ways. We either surrender to them completely and let them pass through us, or we shift attention from one state to another. Thus, the mourner is either encouraged to express his tears and his anguish aloud, or he is directed to the flip side of despair and despondency, which is hope and joyousness. Many people work out some combination of the two.

When the orthodox Jew sits *shiva,* for example, the first three days are days without consolation. Grief is then encouraged to flow. During the following four days, one is not supposed to glorify the deceased any longer. Instead, the emphasis is on the present and the future, in order to distract the family from their loss and reorient them to the world of the living.

Latin American Catholics customarily go through the solemnity of a large funeral procession within twenty-four hours of a death, but afterward will have a fiesta to celebrate the dead one's union with God. Celebrations are the rule in certain Asian countries, for similar reasons. The Irish wake is an outgrowth of the medieval custom of sitting with the dead and enlivening the hours by ribaldry and good spirits—"rousing the ghost"—so as to bring the deceased magically back to life. Gatherings of acquaintances, words of condolence, and baskets of fruit are all intended to succor the living and ease the pain. When religious Jews return from the cemetery they often find bagels and hard-boiled eggs laid out for them, both round forms symbolizing the "rotation of the soul" (*Gilgul Ha'Ne-shama*) which repeatedly goes from the deceased, to heaven, and back again into another body. Both the food and the symbolism are intended for sustenance.

The most essential purpose of the funeral, of course, is the disposition of the body. All manners of disposal have been utilized in the past and present. Certain Indian tribes have left their dead exposed and above ground, letting nature reduce them as she reduces all other forms of expired life. The early Vikings buried their dead at sea. Easterners have favored cremation; Westerners, burial. Aboveground entombments are also employed.

Seventy percent of Americans are buried, making this the

most popular means of disposal. Burnings were foreign to Jewish practice and opposed by early Christians, who viewed this as being instigated by anti-Christs who wished to destroy their belief in the immortality of the soul and the resurrection of the body. This is no longer the case, and cremation now occurs in most of the remaining 30 percent of funerals. Entombment is a relatively insignificant form of disposal in most parts of the country, although a twenty-two-story mausoleum is being constructed in Nashville, Tennessee. And in California, an outfit named Telephase is promoting ecologically sound and inexpensive burials at sea.

If our aversion to death makes us send the dying off to hospitals, so too have we forsaken age-old funeral customs. Undertakers are no longer an option, they are a requirement. Just as custom dictates that men shall wear pants, not dresses, we automatically reach for the yellow pages to find a funeral home when death occurs, instead of burying our own. Even if we wished to do this ourselves—to plant our dead in our own backyards—legislation in most states makes this impossible. In New York, for instance, only a licensed funeral director is allowed to transport a corpse to a disposal site. In our society the undertaker has totally supplanted the family in the preparation of a corpse for burial. Drawing upon skills as a costumer, embalmer, cosmetician, hair stylist, transporter, musical supplier, and chapel arranger, he utilizes sacred rituals yet remains a secular businessman. His services, originally intended to relieve survivors of additional sorrow, are now mandated and serve as a further buffer against a direct experience and a natural acceptance of death. In addition, financial grief is often added to the sadness inflicted by death, since the total cost of the average burial in the United States is more than fifteen hundred dollars.

The American funeral industry has been duly criticized for many of its practices. Jessica Mitford, in *The American Way of Death*, wrote about its high costs, its insincerity, its capitalizing on ignorance and sorrow, and the attempt of too many funeral directors to sell survivors unnecessary procedures and paraphernalia; from embalming to concrete burial vaults designed to protect expensive caskets. It must be said, however, that the fault lies equally with the public, only 28 percent of whom make burial arrangements while alive instead of leaving such costly, confusing, and unsettling tasks to their next of kin. The family, out of guilt or social shame, often feel that elaborate ceremonies are expected of them, that the more money spent atones for any short change they gave the deceased in life. Or they feel that the dead spirit would consider a modestly priced funeral unseemly and selfish.

What makes a funeral so expensive? "Our costs are high," one undertaker told me. "The average funeral director is now a college graduate and demands a salary commensurate with his education. He needs vacations and time off like anyone else. What with back-up men, office overhead, and materials, high prices must follow. Most funeral homes do not do a high-volume business, one director is required for each home, and someone's got to pay for it all."

The undertaker's accounting system is complex. Elaborate itemization makes each charge seem reasonable enough, but the grand total is often staggering. Crematoriums and cemeteries are licensed as nonprofit institutions in New York, as in most states. But the Department of Health licenses funeral directing as a profit-making occupation.

A typical breakdown of costs follows:

IDENTIFICATION OF CHARGES

Member
THE ORDER
OF THE
GOLDEN RULE

A. PERSONAL & PROFESSIONAL SERVICE

1. Transfer of deceased from home, hospital or other — 30
2. Preparation and preservation — 170
3. Grooming and styling hair — 20
4. Restorative operational procedure — 45
5. Personal and staff service for arrangements and supervision — 300
6. Procuring required permits and certificates — 30

TOTAL "A" $ 595

B. FACILITIES & EQUIPMENT

1. Operating room facility — 70
2. Funeral home facilities — 200
3. Service car for local transfer — 25
4. Casket coach for local burial — 65
5. ___ passenger cars at $____ — 55
6. Flower car — 60
7. Transportation outside local area:
   Casket coach to _1.00 PER MILE_ ____
   ___ passenger cars at $____ ____
   to

TOTAL "B" $ 465

C. CASKET AS SELECTED $ 385
155 — 33,830

I. ADDITIONAL MERCHANDISE

a. Outside burial receptacle
   100 – 1,300 (GROUND)
   70 – 1,400 (CREMATE) — 500
b. Burial garments or clothing
   60 — ____
c. Memorial cards — 10
d. Acknowledgement cards — 10
e. ____
f. ____
g. ____

TOTAL I $ 520

II. CASH ADVANCED

a. Opening Grave 75–210 — 150
b. Cremation Fee 100 — ____
c. Clergyman — Church 35–100 — 55
d. Casket Bearers 15/PERSON — 30
e. Newspaper Notices 90¢ to 4.40/LINE — ____
f. Telephone & Telegraph — ____
g. Transcripts of Death Certificate — ____
h. Air or Rail Transportation — ____
i. PURCHASE GRAVE -150-250 — 200
j. ____

TOTAL II $ 435

III. ITEMS ORDERED LATER

a. ____
b. ____
c. ____
d. ____

TOTAL III $ 2,400

We agree to provide services and merchandise as described above.

by_____ License # _____

REMARKS: _____

Although crematoriums charge anywhere from $85 to $100 for a cremation and a five- to ten-minute service in their chapel, the charge in arranging this through a funeral home can come to as much as $1,500. The family avoids such costs as preparation and preservation ($170 for embalming, which is not required by any law and is totally unnecessary unless you fancy sleeping forever in your current physical form), grooming and hair styling ($20), restorative operational procedure ($45), operating room facility ($70), and grave expenses ($350). All other charges are unchanged.

The profit motive operates on all cylinders here. A home may charge $300 for "staff service for arrangements and supervision" and then bill every separate arrangement over again. The attorney general of New York allows an undertaker a 100 percent markup on casket prices over his cost. The cheapest box one can buy costs a minimum of $75, and many homes do not sell them at all. Any carpenter can construct a plain pine box for $30 and still earn carpenters' wages. Caskets, surprisingly, are often required for cremation. And though no undertaker will volunteer it, anyone can legally be buried in a five-dollar shroud, skipping casket costs entirely.

Are there ways to avoid the expense of our elaborate funeral system? There are, but they require advance planning. For starters, one should contact their local funeral or memorial society. Such organizations exist in one hundred twenty cities throughout the United States and Canada. These consist of laymen, and they usually manage to find certain funeral directors who will perform all necessary services for anywhere between 10 to 25 percent of the average funeral fee. Cremations can still be obtained for under two or three hundred dollars in this manner. Burials will of necessity cost a minimum of four hundred dollars more when you add the price of a grave site, the costs of opening it up, and the expense of the simplest marker. Your local society can be found by writing to the Continental Association of Funeral and Memorial Societies, 1828 L Street, Washington, D.C. 20036.

One can also shop around—directly contact various large

and small funeral homes, tell the director exactly what one wants and wishes to spend ("Simple transportation to the crematorium," for example, "in a sack, if possible. And I am prepared to pay a maximum of three hundred dollars.") This too will usually yield results, so that on the date of death a simple telephone call is all that is necessary to complete the funeral arrangements.

* * *

Attending to all the above matters will not only spare the living needless grief, energy, and expense at a time when they are least affordable, but will allow the dying an opportunity to plan and provide for those they love when they are no longer with them. And dying with one's affairs in order is always a whole lot easier.

12

Dying at Home

LONELINESS, DIGNITY, EXPENSE, and home resources are factors to consider when choosing the proper location for dying. There is an erroneous widespread assumption that very sick people should invariably be hospitalized and that the professional care one receives there is superior to that one can get at home. These suppositions, encouraged by physicians and believed by the public, account for the incidence of four people being sent to hospitals when near death to every one who dies at home. Before 1930, death at home was the rule, not the exception.

Hospitals do have their place. They are the location of choice for most people suffering from an acute life-threatening process. Severe trauma, surgical emergencies, and the period of a week following heart attacks, are typical instances where hospital facilities are invaluable. They (as well as nursing homes) can also be useful to the chronically ill who live alone and have no family members or friends willing or able to look after them.

But hospitals are equally abused. Quite often, they serve the economic and convenience interests of the physician rather than the patient. It makes far more sense for a doctor—dollar-and time-wise—to see all his seriously ill patients during one visit to a hospital than it does to travel about town making half a dozen or more house calls. Diagnostic testing might also be carried out on an outpatient basis instead of in hospitals if sympathetic outsiders provide occasional transportation and busy doctors are willing to take the extra time to schedule these procedures. Avoiding hospitalization also avoids the standard hundred-dollar-a-day cost for a semi-private room alone, with doctor's fees and laboratory tests extra.

Though hospitals have sophisticated machinery and trained personnel available to treat critical emergencies, those who work there necessarily lack the personal involvement that is essential for the loving, individual care of the chronically and terminally ill. No private-duty nurse, earning her $47.50 for an eight-hour tour (usually after working a full shift on a crowded ward) can provide that extra degree of alertness and concern that a close friend or family member might. The bed-pan, a change of infusions, an injection of morphine, or a cool towel applied to a perspiring forehead can be supplied as readily by a concerned layman as by a professional.

Like all large institutions, hospitals are invariably bureaucratic, depersonalizing, and isolating. My father, for instance, loved his grandchildren and they him, yet it was against hospital regulations for children to visit. Being a doctor, I man-

aged to smuggle them inside, where they spent mutually re-
warding time together. Most people cannot arrange this.

When people are allowed to terminate their lives in familiar and beloved environments, they have less of an adjustment to make. It is easier to lie in one's own room than to
share semiprivate accommodations with others who may snore,
watch television when you want silence, cry out, or carp about
their miseries. At home, children are frequently involved in
the talk and discussions, and grow up with a viewpoint that
sees death as a natural part of life. In hospitals, such familiarity and casualness are out of the question.

A nurse interviewed by Kübler-Ross expressed a typical
sentiment in talking about the dying patient, about "the ab-
solute absurdity of wasting precious time on people who cannot be helped any longer." It is a well-documented fact that
terminal patients are visited far less frequently by the nursing
staff than those who are expected to recover.

> I am dying with the help of too many
> physicians.
> —Alexander the Great

Physicians and their associates (nurses, orderlies, laboratory
workers) have all but replaced the immediate family as the
new caretakers of the dying. Few of these people have any
intimate relationship with their patients. In contrast to earlier
times, the local practitioner has been replaced by the specialist;
technicians, really, who treat various organ systems and not
the entire person. Add this impersonality to the Hippocratic
mandate that life must be preserved at all costs, and you produce even greater dread. The implication, clearly, is that
death is considered a catastrophe and must be avoided. The
bogus "heroic" last-minute attempts to prolong life—utilizing
support systems ranging from transplants to artificial kidneys,
from heart-lung machines to extremely toxic chemotherapeutic
agents—simultaneously prolong death. Little wonder that those

who have witnessed a relative go through some of these sterile indecencies have marked apprehensiveness when they themselves fall seriously ill.

As a counteraction to such alienating circumstances, new institutions are coming into being. A "hospice" is a place of refuge for those on a journey. Dr. Sylvia Lack, a British physician, is in New Haven, Connecticut, organizing America's first hospice for the dying. Modeled after similar institutions in London, Hospice, Inc, at 765 Prospect Street, intends to provide a humane place to die amid family, friends, and pets, whenever further medical treatment seems pointless. "We are just swamped. Everytime anything about us appears in the newspapers the phone rings all week," she said.

It will be a long time, however, before hospices exist throughout this country. As things stand now, there is no decent alternative to dying in one's own bed. If a fatally ill individual wishes to be hospitalized, that person ought to be, for he or she undoubtedly finds solace in such surroundings. But since most people prefer to die at home, it behooves us to try to make ourselves more available.

If a physician suggests hospitalization when someone you love prefers to remain at home, you must actively question that recommendation. Remember, the doctor has grown accustomed to thinking "Hospitalize the very sick." You must help him consider alternatives, even if these cause him some inconvenience.

There are certain services available that can facilitate home care, particularly when other family members are unavailable to care for the ill. Visiting-nurse services exist in most parts of the country and provide nursing care in an invalid's home. Similarly, homemaking agencies will make someone available to do cleaning, shopping, and cooking when a person is incapacitated. Such agencies can be located in your area by calling your state or municipal health department or social service agency, or by writing to the League of Nursing, 2 Columbus Circle, New York, N.Y. 10019.

Preparations necessary for home care are otherwise quite minimal. A bed can be set up in a spot most convenient for yourself and the ill person. The living room couch is often the site most acceptable. From there, the dying person can participate more readily in the comings and goings of the household, and you can be available to them more easily than if you had to open a distant bedroom door periodically.

You should also locate a medical man willing to make house calls, someone who can prescribe adequate pain relievers if they are needed during the final days. If your family doctor is unwilling to do this and you are not aware of any others, a phone call to your local county medical society will provide you with the names and numbers of those who will make home visits. Many sympathetic physicians would, if asked, readily show a family member how to change intravenous fluids, administer medication, and make the final weeks, days, and hours more comfortable. But first you need to ask.

> Better to die of good wine and good company than of slow disease and doctor's doses.
> —William Makepeace Thackeray

Janet is a fifty-two-year-old, heavy-set, dark-eyed woman just over five feet tall whom I interviewed in her hospital room. Her long black hair, held back with a band, gives her a youthful appearance, despite her years and the gray-and-white striped gown she was issued and wearily wears. Her story is not at all atypical, as she underlines the impersonality, inconveniences, and inadequate pain relief that is often experienced within an institutional setting.

It is unfortunate that she lives in Massachusetts, while her son lives in Florida. Both have separate lives and involvements that they are reluctant to give up. As sick as she is, there is no telling how much longer she might live and Janet does not want to move away from her work or her friends. Thus she has few alternatives to hospitalization when she. feels *in extremis.*

*   *   *

Janet: I had a hysterectomy seven years ago. I didn't know I was supposed to die, so I lived. They put me on some sort of chemotherapy but neglected to tell me that the tumor wasn't benign.

Marty: What were your symptoms then?

Janet: I'm embarrassed to tell you. . . . Promise you won't put it in your book? . . . Oh, I guess it's all right. . . . My diaphragm kept popping out.

Marty: And that was all? No pains? No bleeding?

Janet: That was all. Fortunately, I survived on the medication, but I must have had a relapse several years later. I went back to work, but along the way this anemia came up. My doctor put me in the hospital. They tested me for a nodule on my stomach, which turned out to be malignant. So they did an exploratory procedure, and they found tumors which were inoperable. They were twisted about my liver and several other vital organs. This was five months ago.

Marty: But between these two procedures you felt all right?

Janet: Yes. But this time they told me what it was. I also asked them outright this time. I said, "Look. This time there's no fooling around. I know from the medicine I've been taking that there are several malignancies, and I want to know straight out, how much time have I got?"
He wouldn't be pinned down. But I said, "If I don't respond

to chemotherapy, I want you to tell me. I want to put my house in order." So he said, "Well, if you don't respond, you have about a year." So I said, "Okay, fine."

First they treated me with cobalt, and I responded. I went back to work—too soon, apparently. I worked for two weeks and collapsed. And I came back to the hospital a raving maniac.

Marty: Raving over what?

Janet: The pains in my abdomen were so bad. The cancer cells were really ganging up on me this time. And somebody mentioned that I had a week to live.

But at first I couldn't even get into a hospital. I was running a fever of 103° for a week and my doctor wouldn't come to my house. He figured it was a virus. But I got worse and worse and finally a little incoherent. Finally—I live alone—I called an influential friend who made about forty-five calls and got me into this hospital. It was a tremendous crisis, and if it hadn't been for my friend I would have been gone.

I carried on here for about a week or so because I wasn't getting quite enough medication to suppress the pain. Eventually, some nice young house doctor or intern doubled up on my Darvon, and the pains subsided. Then they began to use a new drug that came on the market only a week and a half before, and it appeared that I was responding to it.

Marty: So in a sense you're in a remission.

Janet: Possibly. And it would be a big surprise to me because I was already planting my daisies. "Put me in this position over here next to my father, on the other side." It was all planned, because I'm not going to live this way.

Marty: How did you know it was so close? Did someone say something to you?

Janet: I just knew. There comes a point when you really know, yourself. And whether you're a big coward about it or not, you say, "To heck with this. Who wants to live this way?"

Once you've adjusted to the idea, you can deal with it. But I'll tell you, for a long time I was very bitter. Not about the illness and the outcome, but the poverty of interest in the disease. They can go up to the moon and pick up rocks and do other things, make weapons and make wars and play with their toys and ballistics. But they don't have enough money for humanity down on earth. I was really mad as hell. And there was no recourse. To whom do you turn?

Marty: You've been in the hospital for how long?

Janet: Three or four weeks.

Marty: And how has that been?

Janet: At first it was terrible. I was in a different room and not getting enough sedation. Then they brought me up here and started regulating me a little better and I calmed down and became the den mother. But they had a very difficult patient in the other corner. There are four beds in each room. She had a very bad thing, too, a benign tumor on the brain. She also had a bad personality problem which you could see had been ingrained for years. She was a very imperious woman and had forty or fifty people visiting her a day. She was very wealthy and they were always kow-towing, bringing her food and sandwiches and meat. And there was never a moment's silence. She was constantly on the phone talking about herself, calling doctors day and night, special nurses giving her baths at ten o'clock at night. Frankly, the surroundings you're in are as important as the medication you receive. I've had two setbacks at other hospitals where I had to go into private rooms because of bad patients in my room. Now these girls [looking around] are wonderful. They've got earplugs to put in their television sets.

Marty: Hospitals are tough places to be treated in. It almost seems better to stay at home.

Janet: But that's tough too. Where do you get people to look after you? My son lives in Florida. And there is no provision for humanitarian needs in this country. I blame it all on political expediency and all the wrong priorities.

Who do you go to in a position like this? If you don't have a million dollars, who do you turn to? I didn't even have a doctor to call. Peculiarly enough, I think that what sustained me more than anything else was my anger. Why the hell do I have to go through this? I'm in the prime of life, at the end of writing a book, the editor was waiting for the final version and I couldn't lift a pencil by that time.

Marty: What do you anticipate in the future?

Janet: I think I'll be going home. I think they'll be giving me someone to take care of me from the American Cancer Society —a homemaker.

Marty: How has your son been taking it?

Janet: Okay. He's visited, although he's in school in Miami. I tell him about these new drugs and also that it's hard to kill a Rockaway Beach kid. That's where I came from. I was raised on broken glass and splinters, and that's a tough background. I was a depression child, so I knew what a struggle was. I was a fighter and still am. Except when you're shadow-boxing, it's not much fun, for you don't know what you're fighting. But I really wouldn't have hesitated to eliminate myself if I had the means. And I have access to the means. I've made sure that if they didn't help me, I was going to say " 'Bye."

I was going to take sleeping pills, because I couldn't take the indignity of drawing out all that mess, you know? The dying and the pain. It was like scissors and knives having a contest. Scythes crisscrossing. They were pretty good and sharp, and varied depending on the sedation.

I still feel that if the pains get unbearable or the treatment excessive, that's it. I think that if people are anxious and really willing to die, they should be allowed to.

Marty: But can't one always do that by refusing medical help and not going in the hospital?

Janet: It's not always that simple. Because if the pain is excruciating, you must go somewhere for help. You can't bear the pain, and you can't even bear the pain to kill yourself, it's that bad at times. You need help to make your way to the exit door.

*   *   *

Helping someone you love to the exit door—instead of leaving that job to others—can be one of the richest personal experiences in both your life and the life that is ending. The dying has a familiar person available to talk with at odd hours, can feel free to make noise, play the radio, raid the icebox, read in the middle of the night, or walk outside for a breath of air without disturbing other patients, the medical or nursing staff, or coming into conflict with hospital rules and regulations. You, the living, will have the satisfaction of seeing your affection expressed in concrete deeds.

Nothing meant more to me than my father's gentle squeezes as we held hands through his last hours. Another friend of mine, Eleanor, saw her husband through a metastatic disease that affected his brain. In the final weeks, he lost his ability to arise. Later, he became unable to walk. Eventually his eyesight failed. She virtually had to provide him with the same care one would an infant.

"When he finally died, I was relieved," she told me. "The efforts exhausted me even with help from my son and some friends. Yet I wouldn't have had it any other way. Mike had periods of lucidity up until the very end, and during those moments a very special and indescribable closeness existed between us. And I was there for those moments, within earshot for his requests, yet free to do my own work."

13

Bereavement

A man's dying is more the survivors' affair than his own.
                                          —Thomas Mann

I GAVE MY SON two baby parakeets for Christmas. Marc had wanted a bird for the longest time. When he saw both of them, his nine-year-old eyes lit up. He thanked me more than once "for the best Christmas I ever had." On trudging up to his room for bed that night, he said, "I'll always remember you for this day," and gave me a rare, unasked-for hug and kiss.

Six days later, one of the birds died—the "one that never bit, who perched on my finger"—the one he liked the most. It had seemed all right earlier in the day but collapsed on New Year's evening, after Marc had fallen asleep. I had promised to wake him at 11:45 to usher in 1975, and I kept my word.

After he rubbed his eyes, we toasted in the year with some beer. Then I told him that I had bad news: his bird had died.

He looked for a moment in wide-eyed silence. Then he bowed his head, his lower lip began to quiver, his face turned red, and silent, copious tears flowed from clenched eyelids. His expression reminded me of every painful moment I have ever felt, and a silent part of me wept too.

I told him how hard it is to lose something you love. He nodded. We passed a few words back and forth and then it was over. It was, after all, only a bird.

The loss of someone you've been close to for years is not as readily settled. Parents, children, husbands and wives all pay a special price when another member of the family dies. Some of these difficulties are practical, some psychological, and all are very, very real.

There is the problem of increased responsibilities. The wife who's lost her husband finds herself forced to deal with a host of new problems ranging from such simple things as car maintenance and home repairs to making financial and business decisions that she had stringently avoided in the past. Husbands whose wives have died must suddenly concern themselves with shopping, cooking, clothing children, attending to their after-school needs, and generally supervising a household.

Financial security is threatened when any parent expires. A housewife can no longer rely on her husband's income. A husband must often hire outsiders to do tasks his wife had performed. There are frequently large medical and hospital bills due and baby-sitters to be hired while grownups evolve new life styles. It all adds up to increased burdens, unshared decisions, and pressures to accept additional roles. Homemaker and businessman, mother and father, are now one and the same

> I'm lonesome; they are all dying; I have hardly a warm personal enemy left.
> —James A. M. Whistler

person. These factors are likely to engender depression and resentment over and above that provoked by death alone.

There is the matter of loneliness, that aching realization which comes upon you in so many different ways and reminds you that someone you shared lives with is no longer about. The simple delights of showing off the new coat you bought, of going to a movie and discussing it afterward, of telling about some small success in life, are gone. If it is a beloved spouse who died, there is no harsher reminder of your loss than facing an empty bed each evening.

There is the tangle of other emotions to contend with as well. In talking about the death of the man in her life, Lillian Hellman put it this way: "I was so often silently angry with Hammett for making the situation hard for me, not knowing then that the dying do not, should not, be asked to think about anything but their own minute of running time." And so one has to deal with their resentments and the self-reproach that follows for having had such typical feelings. Nor is it any easier to deal with guilt.

The mother whose husband has died may feel guilt for not having spent more time with him during his final months and weeks. If she did, there may be guilt for neglecting the children. There is guilt for wishing that the death was over with more quickly, and guilt for occasionally enjoying herself.

> It is foolish to tear one's hair in grief as though sorrow would be made less by baldness.
>
> —Cicero

There are identity problems as the survivor has to redefine who he is and what he wants when his habitual moorings are gone. Finally, there is the dilemma of calmness, the self-suspicions that follow when one adjusts quite readily: "Does it mean I have no feelings? Why aren't I depressed?"

How does one get through this period? Uncertainly. Studies of the bereaved show that they have higher mortality rates, more work problems, and a greater incidence of alcoholism than the general population. Yet there are things one can do to minimize the pain.

Of prime importance is the expression and sharing of feelings before death occurs. In effect, one goes through his mourning period beforehand. There are fewer regrets because things are not left unsaid, and the dialogues you have with the dying can be extremely supportive. Financial matters are settled, alternative living plans are arranged, and there is less of an adjustment to contend with.

This, of course, is not possible when death strikes suddenly. You are left, in such cases, in a state of confusion and have not had time to prepare yourself for your loss.

Here again, one should unashamedly express his honest emotions. Excessive manifestations of tears or laughter might be regarded in poor taste by some, but if they are sincerely felt they ought to be allowed to flow wherever and whenever they happen. Both shake the entire body and provide an excellent release of tension.

It is equally possible that there is no feeling of loss because the relationship was completely satisfying—because the dead person is still with the living in spirit. There may also be no grief because there was no especially important tie. In such cases there is no need to prime the pump, to pretend something that does not exist in order to satisfy social convention or to work toward having the "appropriate" feeling. Whatever you do or do not feel is appropriate and natural for you.

> I have been to a funeral; I can't describe to you the howl which the widow set up at proper intervals.
> —Charles Lamb

My father and I were terribly close, yet I didn't grieve at all when he died. I felt very comfortable about it. Sharing his last moments together, talking through his death spasms, giving him his morphine, and holding his hand was, if anything, a beautiful moment and remains to this day a cherished recollection. Death, when it came, seemed a welcome relief from sickness, and the natural ending to a very full life.

Severe grief is usually related to excessive dependency in the living relationship. If you count on someone as the only depository of your love and hatred or if you are involved in a way in which you need the other person as hopelessly as an addict needs his heroin, you are going to feel profoundly distraught when that person dies. The only way to eliminate this type of bereavement is to strive toward some measure of self-sufficiency before the fact. If it is too late for that, recognize that the anguish you currently feel is akin to growing pains, in ways, and that your loss may eventually represent a gain as you learn to be more independent.

Loneliness is counteracted by the company of others. When you want people about, don't be embarrassed to ask for them. Concepts of "unseemliness" ought to be discarded. Socializing is as necessary a measure as time spent alone.

Activities and tasks are also quite helpful. Having something to do can divert the mind from painful and pointless replays of your loss.

Those who endure a particularly difficult period of bereavement can always consult a therapist. However, as a former practicing psychiatrist myself, I am aware that there are often no shortcuts to the mourning period. But if you can trust the experiences of others, you will gain comfort from the knowledge that the very passage of time itself is healing.

> Everyone can master grief but he that has it.
> —William Shakespeare

Just how one copes with death depends, in large part, upon the personalities of the survivor and the deceased and the quality of the relationship. There are as many tales to be told as there are people, and one can react to someone's death with relief, depression, or tranquillity.

The following accounts are from people who have lived through a death within their family. Regardless of their initial responses, I was impressed by the personal growth of all those survivors I spoke with. Whatever the initial changes each individual went through, all reorganized their lives in an affirmative way, learning through death and maturing through the process of bereavement. Reading their accounts, recognizing that others have navigated these same waters and have felt similar emotions, has to make your own passage just a little easier.

HEE SOO: A YOUNG WIDOW

Hee Soo is a twenty-one-year-old cosmetician who lives by herself in New York. She is a very beautiful Korean woman who radiates self-confidence with her wide and alert eyes, ready smile, and hands that dance as she expresses herself. She has been through two deaths; a recent one involving her husband, and a more remote one, when her grandmother died.

It had always seemed to me that the Buddhist traditions of reincarnation and the scattering of ashes offered the twin comforts of immortality and poetry; that if these concepts existed in the West, death might be less fearsome. And so it was interesting to hear of the fright such traditions can create in Oriental children. It is, perhaps, the task of all children to overcome death anxiety, utilizing modes that make sense to them as they mature.

*   *   *

The first time I met Peter I was in California, attending college. I was seventeen years old and had just come to America. As I walked out of classs one day, I turned my head around and there was a man in a coffee shop across the street. The very same second, he turned his head and our eyes met. It was so unreal. I guess it is what they call "the stars are falling," for I immediately fell in love. It was pure accident.

He was very shy and very nervous. Extremely handsome. All day, the only thing we did was walk and talk, and within twenty-four hours we were married. My parents never knew about it. I could not possibly tell them, with my background and culture.

My father was Catholic and my mother Buddhist. I went to Catholic schools all my life. I spent a year and a half in a convent. Yet, every spring I went to a Buddhist temple to pray for my grandmother.

At the beginning it was very strange. I was a very spoiled, rotten rich kid and he was a struggling racecar driver, trying to get someone to sponsor him. We were married nearly two years and traveled quite a lot. At first we were poor. But when his mother died, he was the only heir to the family wealth, and it was considerable.

The time passed by and then he had his own car. Every Saturday I used to go with him to the track and sometimes would pack a picnic box. I was young and excited about everything. Then, one Saturday, I didn't go. We had an argument and then in the afternoon it happened.

The fight was a stupid little thing. He was overly possessive and jealous. He used to accuse me of things all the time, where I was so innocent and devoted, nothing would ever enter my mind.

We had a friend who was an opera singer, a very handsome young man. I went to market in some store and came back. Peter said he heard the sound of a car that sounded like our friend's, and insisted that he [had] brought me home. I said "No." So he asked, "How did you come home?" I told him my girlfriend dropped me off, but he insisted it was not her car but Norman's. "I know cars, and that was his car." I said, "Well, I am sick of your cars, and if you like your cars so much, go marry your car." I was very upset. Out he went, and I actually laughed.

Later that afternoon someone came over to the house. They told me Peter's car had crashed in the race and he was dead. I didn't react at all. I didn't cry or anything. I was so matter of fact, even laughing, that people must have thought I was really strange. But it was simply because I was totally lost. He was my everything and now I [had] lost everything. I did not know where to go from there.

Peter had seen an analyst for seven years whom I went to see and I stayed with his analyst and his wife over at their house. Dr. Anderson could not figure out how I survived and didn't crack up. For three months I was very ill. I'd get emotional, and I couldn't do anything. After four months I was driving and I had a horrible car accident. It was supposedly my guilt complex. Who knows?

After the car accident I looked horrible. I was hit right in the face. I cried for days and days and days. I could not stop crying. Any little thing, and I would crack up and cry. I could not stand it. I could not talk about his accident or any death at all. I threw away all of Peter's things except for a guitar which he had for twenty years of his life. If I heard anything about him I would start going mad. I didn't want any memories after my car accident, so I came to New York.

I met a man and lived with him for a while, and he was very good, very nice. He was young and good looking, desired by other women, wealthy and all those things. At the time I didn't know left from right. I didn't understand anything. I was still very saturated with what had happened and I guess this man was my nurse. Everybody has their pain, and he helped ease mine. When I left him he hated me for leaving.

Then, finally, everything hit me; all the realness. It took me four and a half months to recognize that Peter was not dead to me. Do you understand how someone could live inside you? I can't explain it at all. I think of him every single day. I have not passed one day without thinking about him, and I am sure this will continue. I visualize things. I think of his expression, smile, certain motions he made, and hear his voice. And I actually smile and laugh and talk back to him. I think, "If I did this, what would his opinion be? I wonder if he would like this?" I carry on conversations with him and I realize "Peter would think this is okay." So he still guides me now.

This was not my first death but my second. The first was worse, because I went through a whole cremation. It happened in Korea when my grandmother died.

I was nine. I saw the body going into a case and smelled the awful odor of flesh burning. It made me nauseous and I had to throw up. That was not all. In a separate room, three monks offer prayers over the body before it is taken for burning. In the casket you put a bunch of flowers and other consecrated things, which at the time I believed in. Monks pray for the soul, and the more money you give them the higher level the soul will go to. That was strange to me, as were all the bodies coming in and out of that room—bodies and caskets going in and ashes coming out. And you smell these bodies burning all the time.

Finally my grandmother's ashes came out and there were some bones left. Very softly, the family picks them up with chopsticks and brings them into another room and they make [them] into an ash. After, we walked up the mountain and spread the ashes all over. Can you imagine how awful that is? Because you are stepping over other ash as you spread yours. And I am thinking, "What does this mean? Someday someone will step on my body?" To me these ashes were bodies. "Is this supposed to be holy?"

Afterward, being a young child, I used to be afraid of death and had all kinds of visions about it. I was not afraid of dying so much as suffocating under the ground if I were buried the Catholic way. And then, from my Buddhist background, I thought of the different animals I might become after death, a human or a bird or dog. And that gave me awful fear. I thought of being a dog and lost in the cold of winter. That seemed to me a most horrible thing. But now I believe that after death my soul will relive, but I don't believe I can explain it.

There are two things in our body. There is the mechanical, physical body; the organs and brains. But what really is living is your soul. These two different things go together right now, but when your physical body dies, your soul goes on. It can go on and on until it finds the right body and enters into another person. People see my outside, but it is my soul that is talking. And that is the revelation that came to me after Peter died.

Everyone has a different response to death. In my case, Peter's dying has been great for me, really, because more good than bad has come from it. I became extremely self-sufficient, disciplined, and I grew as a person. I matured: I've become very beautiful and self-confident knowing that I could live through that and have lived through that and done so well after his death. I feel that I can attempt anything, and that is what makes me become very egotistical.

*   *   *

Hee Soo's dialogues with her dead husband do not in any way signify psychopathology. They are instead her way of incorporating what Peter stood for, for reminding herself of values and judgments of his that are important to her in the present time.

Knowing how well she functions in life, how level-headedly and positively she thinks, I can only agree that she has, indeed, matured through her very real loss.

DAVID: A SINGLE PARENT

David is a school teacher who lives in a large tenant-managed apartment house in Chicago. The father of three, his soft voice and fine features give him an air of intensity and introspective sensitivity.

His story underscores the difficulties of social readjustment when a spouse dies, as well as the importance of activities to make the time of grieving and transition more tolerable.

* * *

It was a year ago that Janet entered the hospital for two operations. One was to remove stretch marks off her stomach and one for a nose job. Her nose was almost perfect. The stretch marks were visible, but they were never a concern to me. I think her desire for cosmetic surgery stemmed from childhood when she was rather heavy and unhappy. It wasn't until college that she really thinned down and apparently gained confidence in herself. But I imagine those early years were too much for anyone. As many times as marriage was proposed to her it never convinced her that she was pretty.

She really didn't need the operations, and it was obvious that they were costly. But she said that she was working, and it was hard to argue against that. So she went into the hospital just about a year ago, on the eighteenth of December. The operations were scheduled to take place on the nineteenth and twenty-first so that she would have the Christmas vacation to recuperate. They were both minor operations. The first procedure was performed on Wednesday and all went well. That was on her stomach. The nose job was set for Friday morning.

I got over to the hospital about 1:00 P.M. expecting to see her back in the room. My mother-in-law came in shortly thereafter and we were waiting. It seemed rather unusual that such a simple operation would be delayed, but I didn't know much about operations. We asked nothing and nothing much was told to us. Sometime between 2:00 and 3:00 P.M., a nurse came out and said, looking away from us, that the doctors would like to see me downstairs. My first reaction was that they fucked up, that they had botched the nose up and wanted to explain to me how; you know, some complication but nothing serious.

I was taken into this little office. Her doctor and his associate sat me down. One of them told me that she reacted to the

cocaine packing that they put in the nose, that she had a cardiac arrest, and that she was dead. I was dumb-struck. I didn't
break down. I asked "How could it happen?" and "How
did you let it happen?" Before I finished asking questions,
they were saying they tried all they could—did all they could—
all that bullshit.

Janet was in the prime of health. She was looking better
than she ever had and she was really into a lot things, active
and working. I didn't have great anger. I didn't hit a cabinet.
I was reasonably cool. Then I went up to get my mother-in-law
and broke the news to her. We then called Janet's father and
other relatives who had to know. Not too long afterward my
father-in-law and Janet's brother arrived, along with his future-
father-in-law, who is an attorney and initiated the funeral arrangements. We were just working, separated from the whole
thing, doing these tasks and not having any time to experience
what had actually happened. Then they drove me home. My
father was there with his brother and his brother's wife, taking
care of our kids.

My feelings were that I was sorry that I had not done more
when she was alive. That was my first feeling. It was remorse
that I could have done more and now there was no time to
do it. I could have been a better husband, been nicer and more
appreciative.

By then there were many people around, and we spent that
first evening together. My father stayed with me for a few
days. The following day, since it was an unusual event, there
were legal proceedings and we had to go to the coroner's
office, have an autopsy performed, and identify the body. The
hospital was already beginning to create their own story, their
lies in preparing for whatever they knew was going to happen. Then we went out to make the final funeral arrangements.
That evening, at the chapel, tons of people came. Janet's very
popular. The following day the funeral was held. Again there
was an overflow of people.

My children at that time were nine and a half, eight, and

four. The oldest boys I could talk to, so I told them about Janet's death that same afternoon. They didn't say much. They cried a bit and that was very touching. The Christmas presents were all set out and I let them open the presents. I knew it would be easier to tell them than to tell my youngest. He was going to nursery school at that time and was staying with a woman who was a very lovely person who takes kids in. I knew that when he returned, things might be said. He should know, but I really was hesitating. I delayed.

I can't define it, but I knew it would be very hard for both of us. He is a very special kid. Anyway, it was three, four, five days later—I don't remember exactly when—that the woman who watches him came up one evening and what she said had a great impact on me. She said she felt it was best for him if I told him as quickly as I could, and I decided I had to tell him the next morning. I didn't come out with it the way I should have, really. But I said mommy had gone to the hospital and that she was not going to come back. The look on his face was as if he had been stunned by a bolt. Then he lay on the floor and cried a bit. That scene was something I will never forget.

Six or seven months later, without too much assistance from me, he put it into place. For many many months he said his mother was sick and I would begin to say "No," but I just didn't have the heart or courage to explain. Anyway, almost on his own, from the things he heard from others, he worked it out that his mother was dead. He is an unusual kid and he adjusted to it by himself at the age of four. But as far as my kids were concerned, they never really wanted to know the details and they still don't.

For my kids, the saving factor was just living in this building. So many friends live here that their lives didn't change too much. Other kids were there and their school and their things. And of course I am always home. I get home early enough and I have always taken care of them a lot, so the whole pattern was not really drastically altered. I really don't know the impact it's had on the oldest to this day. They seem quite the same.

At first I got concerned about them. When I initially tried to bring up the subject they would try to shut me out. I went so far as to call a psychiatrist. My biggest question in going to him was to find out if it is normal for them to shut off like that. He said that as far as he knew he didn't think it was so unusual, and that relieved my fears. I didn't return to him.

There were many times I would cry, but I cried to myself, thinking it would be best. In retrospect, I'm not so sure. Who knows? The reason I think it might have been better to grieve openly is that if they would have seen those feelings in me, it might have given them license to get the same feelings out, to know that it was a very shattering experience.

The most important thing was having people around; just being able to be with other people in the evenings, especially. I'd never felt very social before, but I just could not be alone. And people were very kind and very considerate and helpful, and everybody wanted to do everything.

It hit me very often when I would come home in the afternoon and the kids would go out and play. I never felt really depressed in my life for maybe more than a day or a half-day or an hour. Now I knew what depression was. Not that I was really out of it. I was working and I started to jog in the afternoons, two or three times a week. Between running and showering, the afternoon passed, and then in the evening I would go downstairs and visit a neighbor. It helped to keep busy. Work was good for me.

With Janet gone, I now had more work to do: cleaning, cooking, making a sandwich and such. It is time consuming and wearing, but I knew I could handle it because I had handled it. Fortunately, the rent here was okay. Finances were really not a problem. Eventually I was able to file for Social Security, which a person should do if the other partner had been at work. There is a certain payment for each dependent child. In my case it came to $395 per month.

The days passed. At first it was very hard going back to work knowing that I would have to listen and talk with all those people saying their thing to me. It revives certain feelings in you. It touched certain nerves and kept up the intensity of my sorrow. Sitting in the cafeteria with fifty to one hundred people and knowing many want to come over to you and talk is a little hard. But it was not as bad as I anticipated once I was there. Everybody was very nice and thoughtful, and the patterns of life resumed. Work on the job and work in the home and quite a number of people visiting all helped.

As the days passed, I began to feel the need for a woman. It must have been swelling up, for I didn't realize it taking hold. Some friends suggested that I go to an encounter session and let things out and also possibly meet people. I did go down two times but somehow I wanted to do it myself. I did, though, realize that I was thrown into a new world. Suddenly I was single, and I knew I would have to play a different ballgame. Just going to the car or taking a trip to see old friends yourself can be a difficult thing. For twelve years, when I would get dressed to go out, I would usually be going out with Janet. Here I was doing it myself. Things like that always provoked sadness . . . sadness for myself.

Anyway, I had never gone out with too many women. I was just starting. I dreaded the thought of having to go to singles bars. I went once and it was a disaster. Yet I was prepared to try all ends, for I did want to meet someone who could turn me on.

If I were trying to help others, I would say that they should seek companionship from members of the opposite sex as soon as they can. I can't give any recommendations as to how to do it. I wanted to go out, but I was reluctant to do it too soon. I was mostly concerned with whether there was a proper time or a proper time not to; with what people might say, particularly my father-in-law. He had lost his first wife and then lost his daughter. I really felt terribly sorry for him, too, and I didn't want to do anything that would make him think less of me.

But he didn't have to know nor did he ask, so it wasn't difficult to not infringe on his feelings.

I went to a few Parents Without Partners parties, but it was not for me. They were too old. I went to a church which also has a singles set-up. That wasn't too bad, and I met someone there who was quite nice.

I could see possible harm coming from running out of the house. I know I have to feed my boys and get them up in the mornings. If I had a date, which most often involves dinner, I would have to leave home early. Since they had not had a sitter for a while, just arranging to get out was difficult. There would be a lot of extra yelling. I would be leaving them. I was selfish and I wasn't sure whether I should go, although they were used to being left alone. Now that there was only one person around to return, I felt badly about it. Yet I had to go out. It might have become a source of friction, but again, it didn't materialize, because I met Carol.

She invited me and my children over to supper sometime late in March. I had very strong feelings for her and it seemed to be mutual. We went away for Easter together and got along terrifically. We saw each other more and more and began to talk about living together. We decided to live together as of the end of September. It is now the end of November and there is no way I can tell anyone how to work that out, but it just happened. Maybe part of it was my great need to have somebody, but I can't believe I would have gone out and grabbed the first person. There was a very strong attraction. She was able to provide me with the things I needed.

With her two and mine at home there is a great deal of fighting. Five boys. But I believe even five brothers would fight. I guess it's not too bad. They seem to get along pretty well. Fortunately there's room here. My youngest needs a woman in the house. I try to be pretty much the same with my kids. I may have bought them a few more things than I ordinarily would have, but day-to-day relationships are pretty much the same. I try to give them a lot of time.

Once in a while, when I take a look at my youngest kid, who is sort of special, I have a feeling of sadness that Janet will miss so much of him and sorrow that so much of her life—which was just reaching a prime—is gone. I also know that I have learned a lot in retrospect, and I hope that I will be able to use what I have learned to help make an even better relationship with Carol. I know more readily my faults and weaknesses, and in being aware of them at least I have something to work on.

* * *

The great remorse, David reminds us, came from his not having expressed his full appreciation for his wife while she lived. Her sudden death prevented him from resolving this issue. David also touches on many of the problems faced by young parents who lose a spouse, on the difficulties in telling children, of running a household, of their longings for a new mate and their concern as to how this natural desire will seem to others.

The children, of course, do better than the parent expects. The four-year-old's early insistence that his mother is just sick is a normal response, as children that age don't realize death is a permanent condition. And David's visit to a psychiatrist reassured him, for the therapist affirmed the rights of children (people) to react to their mother's death in their own way—less forcefully than their father anticipated.

The drudgery of the dating game comes through in this account, as it does for all those who attempt it after living with someone for years. Did David involve himself with Carol as an escape from this scene? Was she simply a good compromise? Who knows. And who is to say whether compromises aren't perfectly valid means of coping. I prefer to think of their meeting as one of those kindly interventions of fate, for I met Carol when I met David. She is as he describes her—quite attractive and very desirable. Given his new recognition of his faults in relationships, David has a chance to make this union even more meaningful than the one he lost.

LINDA: LOSING A SISTER

Linda is a friend of mine, a twenty-four-year-old woman who teaches dance at a Montessori school. Small in stature, she is large in temperament and has, in the past, presented herself to the world with a contentious outspokenness softened by a playful teasing and flirtatiousness. Dark haired and dark eyed, her usual testiness is gone and she seems to be a much softer person since the death of her sister less than two months ago.

Her story highlights the inadvertent guilt that many survivors feel for not having acted differently; the feeling that if they had taken proper steps, a life would have been spared. There is also a clear articulation of the process of identification with the deceased, where she felt, at times, that she and her sister were one.

*   *   *

My sister was the closest person to me. She took me places, introduced me to art, culture, everything in New York City. As I got older we suddenly became friends, started to do things on the same level, and went through a new world together—so many transitions together.

She had diabetes, but many people live long lives with diabetes. Otherwise she was perfectly healthy. A month and a half ago, when she was thirty, she decided she wanted to raise a family with this new man. She spent $175 for a wedding dress and got a new apartment. The night before her wedding she died. It was a total shock and happened because the doctor made a foolish mistake.

A couple of days before the wedding I spent the evening at her house. I went because she was not feeling very well. She didn't say it was very bad, but she did say she was in a lot of pain and was retching all day. Finally, we called a doctor. He diagnosed it as hysteria, although a first-year medical student should have known she had symptoms of acidosis [a diabetic crisis], which consists of heavy panting and pain all over the body. "Is she a very exuberant person?" he asked. "Does she get excited about her wedding? Stay with her all night. It's hysteria. I will give you 100 milligrams of Seconal. She will be a little groggy in the morning, but she will be okay." You never knock out a diabetic, because they are supposed to tell you how they feel.

She didn't know what to tell the doctor. All she said was, "I am in a lot of pain. I took an insulin injection." She continually got worse and worse through the night. Finally, we called an ambulance. We got her to the emergency ward in the hospital. Her heart stopped twenty minutes after we arrived, for about six minutes, but they got it working again. Then she went up to intensive care and was placed on the critical list. She was there for a day and a half. They called in heart specialists, surgeons, and others. They kept telling my father that "we are trying everything we can, but it is not too hopeful." And then she died.

A couple of minutes after my sister-in-law called me and said "she didn't make it," I hung up the phone. I went to my bed and started crying. I looked in the mirror and I saw her.

Later, I saw her when she was lying in bed with all the tubes attached to her, and I was debating whether I wanted to see her dead or not. I had been sorry that I had not seen my mother dead. But I didn't go to see her, because I had a couple of conferences with the family and I decided I wanted to remember her alive. They were very shocked that I would want to see her after she died. They said, "Don't be silly." I grew to believe from our conferences that she was no longer there; just a shell was there, and I would be seeing her shell, which I could see as readily on photographs. Part of her was inside me now, and suddenly the expression "Someone lives in your heart" was no longer a cliché to me, because I really felt her inside me.

She was having an orthodox Jewish wedding, so we believed she would have wanted us to sit *shiva* [a custom of gathering together for a week to honor, pray for, and mourn the dead]. I really thought at first I wouldn't make it. I felt totally alienated from my family. I felt as if I were dealing with death differently from anyone. My brother-in-law was playing backgammon. I would be insulted by it and then I realized that was his way of handling it. So that was part of sitting *shiva*. I had never done it before, and I learned you have to cover all the mirrors in the house. It suddenly dawned on me, "God. This is great." Because I was getting freaked out everytime I looked in the mirror. They say you have to let the spirits pass over and you can't be vain the week of sitting *shiva*. I really felt the truth in that.

I felt extreme guilt for not calling an ambulance at first instead of listening to the doctor. The doctor looked like the kind you would have seen in a movie. A perfect young doctor with a French accent, very suave, who said things definitively. However, after a while, after hours went by, I would say to my sister-in-law, "We should really get an ambulance." My sister-in-law would say, "No. Let's listen to the doctor." I felt it would be selfish to trust my own intuitions. I should trust this doctor with twelve years of experience. He learned the field. I should trust him. But I just . . . I felt so guilty after the whole thing. Afterward I found out that the point at which I wanted to call the ambulance was already too late, that she was so far gone it was unlikely they would have saved her anyway. So that alleviated my guilt.

The funeral was remarkable. It seemed there were millions of people. And the eulogy was incredible. She knew a rabbi very well. She was his student and he was her student. He lived in Boston and flew in. He never did a eulogy in his life, but he did this one. He made me believe that quality was more important than quantity, and that the way she lived for thirty years, most people don't live in ninety. At the funeral me, my twin sister, and my father were just arm in arm, linked for hours, wailing. The rabbi was relating a lot of things that she was doing before she died. She was about to edit a book. Harper & Row had given her an advance and she was putting together a compilation of writings by Jewish women, including her own.

I suddenly think it's almost as if I am borrowing her strength. I feel as though life is more precious and I must live to the fullest and not waste time, because I could die at thirty, too. I also felt grateful for the first time in my life to the Jewish religion, which created such a way for handling death immediately afterward, in which the whole family sits together in one room and not only mourns, but we laughed hysterically. We told jokes. We did everything to get the feelings out, and I took the week off from work. When I came out, it was like adapting to a world I had never known before—reattaching.

The fact that my boyfriend could make out with my girlfriend right in front of me was trivial. Death and life seemed like the only important things to me, and I just felt that I had to go on living, and so I will. The week after I stopped sitting *shiva* I felt very up, very alive, very beautiful, and thankful to be alive.

The first day back on my job there were fruit baskets waiting for me and Welcome Back signs all over the place. It was a nice transition, and they made me feel loved. The children were so spontaneous and so direct about things. They would come over to me and say things like "Your sister died? Why did she die?" and I would tell them. That made me face up to it more as an everyday occurrence because they accepted it and didn't crack up when I told them she died.

Right now I'm much more appreciative and less petty about things. Like what I said about my boyfriend. Or concerning material possessions. I'm less concerned if I look good or not as opposed to if I feel good or not. I'm being less impulsive financially and trying to get my money trip together. I am going through individual therapy now with a woman and I am taking it more seriously. I want to get out of it as soon as possible because I'm paying ten dollars a session and I don't want to pay for something like this. I don't go there just to bullshit. I go there to get something out of each session and I am procrastinating a whole lot less. And I'm telling people more directly the good thoughts I have about them. Because they might not be here tomorrow.

*   *   *

It is unfortunate that her family did not support Linda's initial desire to see her dead sister. This is typical of the aversion so many people feel for death, regardless of the rationalizations they use as a cover story. We do, though, see the variability of emotions displayed through the mourning ritual of sitting *shiva,* as well as the cleansing effect such discharge of expressions has.

Notwithstanding her feelings of guilt, Linda's development through her sister's death is obvious. She has used it to motivate herself to do and say things now and not postpone words and actions for a tenuous and uncertain future.

DEBORAH: A HUSBAND'S SUICIDE
AND DAUGHTER'S DEATH

Deborah is a short, matronly looking woman of thirty-eight who in less than a year lost both her husband and a daughter. The differences between these deaths are marked, for one was a relief and the other a deep loss.

We see how one family copes with suicide and the bitter feelings from which some suicides arise and which they perpetrate. As in the other stories, we bear witness to the ephemeral nature of life; the abruptness with which it passes.

*　　*　　*

My husband committed suicide. I don't think I ever really considered the thought that he would. He was having problems and would talk about going away somewhere and chucking everything. And he had started to drink heavily. He was a physician and he took an overdose of Seconals after drinking.

Our marriage was on the rocks. Probably his death was more of a relief than anything else. Not that I wanted to see him dead, but everything was in such a state at that time. He had a girlfriend who was about to give birth and I think that was what he could not face. She gave birth about three weeks after he died. We had been married for seventeen years, had three children, and each reacted very differently to what happened.

He was never a happy person. No matter what he did, it was always the wrong thing as far as he was concerned. He could never make a decision, and therefore I was put into the position of making all the decisions. But any decision I made was always the wrong one too. So no matter what anybody did, it was wrong. One week he would be contemplating folding up his medical practice here and moving somewhere else, and the next day he would be looking for another office here in Boston.

When he told me about the situation with this woman who happened to work for him, I didn't explode. Maybe if I had he would have felt better about it. I sort of accepted it and said, "Well, it happened. Do you want to leave? Do you want a divorce?" He said no, we would work it out. At first he said, "Oh, how wonderful. You're marvelous to act this way." Then he got very angry with me. Maybe he felt that I didn't care because I didn't start screaming all over the place.

Then one night he didn't come home at all, never called in at the hospital, and the answering service had not found him. I finally remembered that he had a key to a friend's apartment. I called the hotel at about six in the morning. There was no direct line to the room. I had to go through the switchboard, and they said it was impossible for anybody to be in the room without their knowing, and they refused to check. Later on in the morning, my friend, whose husband's room this was (they are separated) came over and I said, "Look. You call. It's your husband's room. Maybe they will do something for you." She called and finally someone did go up and they found him dead.

He left notes. The note to me was not very nice. When I read it I was very upset, hurt, and angry. It said that I never loved him and now I had what I wanted, money, and I should never enjoy it.

He left a note to his parents saying that he always blamed them for his problems, but he knows it was not completely their fault. It implied that he was still blaming them. And to the children that he was taking a grand cop-out and they should never do the same thing; that he tried to find love at home and could not do so, so he looked for it elsewhere. And he left a note, I assume, to his girlfriend. I don't know that he wrote to her, but he left the note for her lawyer, and in that note he asked that part of the money from the life-insurance policy go to her to care for the baby. I had a problem on my hands because of that. The insurance company would not give me that money until it went to court and got settled—for a much smaller amount than he had stated in his note, but for her it was still quite good.

My children were eleven, thirteen, and fifteen at the time. They reacted very badly. My youngest one was at camp and I sent my brother up there to bring her home. We did not tell her at camp why she was coming home, but I understand from the camp director that she spent her last moments at camp crying and was sure that something had happened to her father. When I asked her later why she thought that, she said because when she talked to us on the telephone she could hear everybody else in the background but could not hear him. When she did come home and was told, she asked, "Why did you bring me home from camp? I could have stayed there." And she never reacted to it again.

My oldest one treated it as if nothing had happened. When I asked her why, she said, "It was just as though he didn't exist anyway. He left us a long time ago. What difference does it make?" It affected my middle one the most. She fought with him constantly. They were very much alike in temperament. She had had a fight with him a few days before this happened, and her sisters also made her feel that maybe she drove him to this. It was unfair to do this to her, and she reacted terribly. She went from being an A student to not going to school and almost flunking everything. She refused to go for help then, and still won't. She transferred schools. She decided that she wanted to be Catholic, I think as a means of being closer to her father, even though he wasn't a practicing Catholic. He was raised as one but never considered himself anything. But she wanted to go to a parochial school, so I figured that if this would make her happy, fine. Anyway, she is going to parochial high school now, and she got her first report card and did very well. But she is still emotionally upset and she could really use the counseling.

So his death resolved a terrible marriage; one I never would have ended, though, as it would have been admitting failure. That was the main reason. And he always said if we ever separated he would not support me. He would just leave. I would not have done that, for it would have been hard living alone without an income from him.

I had taught on and off, but I did not like teaching. I had pre-med courses in college, but I married when I graduated instead of going to medical school, which I should have done. I sat home and read medical journals. That's why it upset me when he complained that he had to go out on calls, because he was doing what I wanted to do and he was bitching about it. But with him dying, I had enough money to go back to school, which is what I'm doing now. I'm taking a doctorate in psychology and plan to be a therapist. And I don't have to be dependent on my parents at this time. I am financially comfortable. Raising children by yourself is still a burden, but that would be true under any circumstances.

Of course, his death caused me many problems in addition to the ones it ended. My children were used to having a mother at home that didn't work, one they could call. "Mommy wash this. Mommy do that." Mommy spent her life with all of her children, and now Mommy is going to work and going to school and dating and they didn't like it. They still don't like it. I have my hands full, especially with the little one. She wants everything to go back to the way it was.

I discussed it with my therapist and he said, "If you stay home, you will become bitter and that will be worse for them than anything else." So I could not do it. I had to survive. But sometimes it was very difficult.

When my husband died, my oldest daughter, who had been

very introverted most of her life and had not really confided in me or in her father, felt a weight was lifted from her. She started to change and became much more open, much closer to me, and we were able to talk to each other. She became much friendlier with other kids her age. She had not really had any friends for a period of time and she was not doing anything. She'd come home from school and sit and watch television. She had always been bright, but there was also a period of time when she was not doing too well. She was cutting and playing hooky. And when her father died, she suddenly started hitting the books and got a ninety-four average. She just started to change completely. Where the middle one started to fail everything and became completely emotional, Janie seemed to bloom.

After half a year, everything was getting to a point where we were adjusting to the fact that there were four of us in the family, and we had to do certain things that we didn't do before. Everything was calmed down and I took the kids on a vacation down in Florida during February. That was the first time I had taken them anywhere, and we had a very nice time. When we came back, Janie was busy with school, making a costume for a play she was in. And then, in late March, after a performance of the play, she collapsed. They called my house. I was at the office. The other two children were at home and they needed permission to treat her. Cheryl, my middle one, gave them my in-laws phone number, and they gave permission and rushed off to the hospital. Of course, the two kids were frantic. They did not know what had happened. I got home about one hour after this occurred.

I rang the doorbell, but all I could hear was Cheryl screaming, and I thought they were fighting with each other. I didn't know what happened. She opened the door and just kept yelling, "Janie's dying, Janie's dying," and all I could think of was that maybe the kid had gotten into a car and had an automobile accident or something. I did not know what. I asked what happened. She said, "Janie's dying. She collapsed at school and is in the hospital." I just grabbed her and we got into a cab and ran over.

I called a friend of ours who is a doctor. He is not on the staff but a resident there told him that there was a slight chance that she would live 'til morning. I just didn't know what was happening. I think I was in shock.

Janie had a slight cold and had come into my room that morning to say, "So long." She was fine. I have a picture of her that was taken two hours before she collapsed from a cerebral aneurysm. They said it must have been something she was born with and it just worked thin and broke.

She never came out of the coma. They tried to talk me into letting them take away the respirator, but I wouldn't. They also called me and asked me to donate her kidneys and things like that. But I couldn't bring myself to do it. If it had been done differently maybe I would have, but I didn't like the way it was done. The whole situation in the hospital was a nightmare. It would have been a nightmare anyway, but . . . toward the end, they wanted her out of the intensive care unit and tried to force me to put her into a private room.

She was there for three and a half weeks. It was a constant barragement aside from the fact that I knew my daughter was dying. The people around the hospital were saying, "She cannot stay here. We need the bed." There were other beds in the intensive care unit and I knew enough about hospital procedure. I believe where there is life, no matter how slight it is, something can happen. I wouldn't want anyone to pull the plug on me.

Anyway, one night—it was April twentieth—I got a call that she had taken a turn for the worse and I should come to the hospital. I knew she was dead at that point, because I knew hospital procedure. My little one didn't want to come. I took Cheryl with me. Janie had died a couple of hours before. I really don't know what the exact cause of death was at that moment. I have never gotten an autopsy report, though she had developed pneumonia.

During this whole period of time, everybody around me went crazy. First of all, I had my parents staying with me. My mother couldn't keep from crying the entire time and my father wasn't well as it was. It was a very big burden having them there. Cheryl was not going to school. She spent a great deal of time at the hospital. Ellen didn't come to the hospital. She just carried on as if nothing was wrong, just as she had when her father died. Everybody wanted to help me. Nobody could. I wanted to help everybody else. In any type of grief, in the long run, you are alone, and no matter how other people try, they cannot help. They sometimes just make it worse.

I don't like being comforted. I don't mind someone being there and letting me baby myself and cry or whatever. But I cannot stand being patted and hearing "Everything will be all right," because everything won't be all right. I want to get it out of my system. Just don't say things that you don't mean or that you're saying just to comfort me. It only hurts more.

Anyway, I had no time to get hysterical, because everybody else around me was. I finally broke down after it was all over, and then I was with a friend. We were talking about college and he inadvertently asked, "How much does it cost to send three kids to college?" He said "three kids" instead of two, and that was it. I cried for about five and a half hours. I finally cried myself to sleep, and it still doesn't seem quite real. She's not here but I can't say I feel as if she's gone.

Things will happen, and I still feel like crying. I don't think about it for a while and then I will see someone or I will keep getting notices from college addressed to her. Cheryl reminded me that it was six months on the twentieth since Janie's death. They miss her. Most of the time when they talk about her they talk as though she were still alive. I can't even think of some of the silly things they say.

My experiences with the suicide was, I guess, not the same as everyone's, because at that point I really didn't care anymore. You hurt so much, and my future was so uncertain, that I really didn't react to it with sorrow. I think the biggest thing to remember is that the only person responsible for someone committing suicide is the person who commits suicide. You cannot keep anyone from killing themselves.

Losing a child, I think, is the worst thing that could happen to anybody. I don't know. The grief is there and there is nothing you can do about it—just sort of live around it—get back into life. It never goes away, but you learn to accept it. Life goes on. It just doesn't stop, and if you dwell on that, it's just a loss of that one life and a loss to the people around you. It is not fair to yourself or anybody else. There are other things that you can do. It frightens me, of course, that it could happen again. There is just no guarantee that it won't.

My own attitude about life has always been that I want to enjoy it and I would never, never think of killing myself, because I don't know what's going to happen tomorrow. It might be something fantastic. That has always been my attitude. I don't think it's changed.

* * *

Again we see a great variability in reactions to death. Deborah grieves for her daughter and feels nothing for her husband. One child, Janie, reacts positively to her father's death, and Cheryl takes a nose dive.

We also see different ways of coping. Deborah finds support through a therapist who encourages her to live for herself. Cheryl recoups through transfering to a parochial school.

This unpredictability of response is what makes one reluctant to offer specific formulas as to how best to cope, beyond urging each person to do and pursue those activities that offer comfort and support regardless of the forms they take.

Most of all, though, we see a wise woman who is able to transcend grief, get on with living and retain, in spite of her twin confrontations with death, a basically optimistic orientation toward life.

14

Meditations

DEFINITIONS OF DEATH

The port where all may refuge find.

—William Alexander

A release from the impressions of the senses, and from desires that make us their puppets, and from the vagaries of the mind, and from the hard service of the flesh.

—Marcus Aurelius

The blessing which men fly from.

—George Henry Boker

187

The grand perhaps.

—Robert Browning

The liberator of him who freedom cannot release, the physician of him whom medicine cannot cure, and the comforter of him whom time cannot console.

—Charles Caleb Colton

A law, not a punishment.

—Jean-Baptiste Dubos

The goal of all life.

—Sigmund Freud

A tavern on our pilgrimage.

—John Masefield

The undiscover'd country, from whose bourne no traveller returns.

—William Shakespeare, *Hamlet*

When two worlds meet with a kiss: this world going out, the future world coming.

—Talmud, *YeBamot* 15.2

CONTEMPLATIONS

1.

My middle son, Richard, is a gifted artist. When he was five years old, I put together a book with a series of his drawings and accompanying captions. It was filled with all sorts of things relating to death: vampires and monsters and Frankensteins. When I read his book to other kids they would invariably be turned on by the killings, excitement, and their attempts to comprehend and deal with their fears of death.

When the book was shown to publishers they'd say, "Oh. Children aren't interested in that. Death is a distasteful topic."

That is part of the Conspiracy of Silence that works to keep people intimidated by the subject.

2.

Where is the horror in informing someone that he is dying? Aren't we all dying from the moment of our birth?

3.

My father's dying of cancer totally changed my ideas about that illness. He was told what he had, and the knowledge didn't sour his remaining days.

Cancer is the one disease that everybody tries to frighten you about. When the American Cancer Society wants to raise money, they scare you with the idea of cancer. I now think that cancer can actually be a pleasant way to die. Perhaps words like "pleasant," or phrases like "death can be your friend," are exaggerations, "pleasant" meaning "it has advantages over other forms of death," "it can be your friend" meaning "it can be an exciting inner experience."

For instance, cancer is a slow going away. You can leisurely take care of your affairs, converse with close friends and family, and wrap up much unfinished business. You can die a lot differently, stylistically, of cancer than you can by dying in an auto accident or having a cerebral blood vessel burst.

I would no longer mind dying of cancer, for I feel it would allow me to watch myself, more fully, as I go.

4.

None of us will ever get out of this world alive.

5.

The more I have thought of the concept THE END, the more absurd it seems. How can we have an ending when we cannot conceive of our beginning?

When did you begin?

When you said "Momma" for the first time?

When you cried and took your first breath in the delivery room?

When you kicked the inside of your mother's womb when she was five-months pregnant?

When you were first conceived?

Was that when you were first turned on? Is that micro-photograph of a newly fertilized egg your first baby picture?

And where were you before then? You were split into two parts. Part of you was suspended in your father's testicle and another dwelt in the ovary of your mother. So you existed in them, even though they didn't know it at the time and you don't remember it at all.

They, of course, went through the same process. That means that you were split into four when we go back to your grandparents. And if we go back far enough—through our most distant great-grandparents and the creatures that existed before them—it is plain that you can confirm your existence since it all began.

6.

Our consciousness is not likely ever to be destroyed, for consciousness exists in every bit of matter within us. And whatever becomes of us, the matter of which we are composed goes on existing. The old divisions of animate/inanimate, living/dead are obsolete concepts.

I heard of one experiment in which semen from various donors was placed in vials in a laboratory. When any given donor stepped into the room, the sperm cells within only his vial responded by showing heightened motility.

Does a white blood cell traveling about within our body meet, eat, and digest an invading bacterium because we command it? Or does it do so under its own initiative—its own consciousness—because it has a yen for that type of food?

Nothing in the scientific developments of his lifetime so dismayed the young Albert Einstein as the evidence that atoms had apparent consciousness and could not individually be described in cut-and-dried, cause-and-effect terms. In a letter he wrote to Hedwig Born* in 1924 he said, "The idea that an electron ejected by a light ray can choose *of its own free will* the moment and direction in which it will fly off, is intolerable to me. If it comes to that, I would rather be a shoemaker or even an employee in a gambling casino than a physicist."

Yet the behavior that Einstein found intolerable continues to exist. Individual atoms can still be shown to emit particles, light waves, or other forms of radiation at unpredictable times, in unpredictable directions, and with no discernible immediate cause.

---

*The wife of the German physicist Max Born.

7.

"People can't sleep forever."

"Nobody can die and come back to life."

"Reincarnation is strictly superstition. You only live once."

So common sense tells us. Years ago, I came across a line written by a nineteenth-century French philosopher whose name escapes me. Yet it so appealed to my common sense that I could not forget the author's message:

"To be born twice is no more amazing than to be born once."

8.

What if we don't remember a time before our flesh-and-blood existence?

Does a butterfly remember its former existence as a caterpillar?

9.

Actually, the idea of living forever is consistent with twentieth-century science, since the body can never witness its own passing. In that sense, life goes on eternally.

Events are perceived through the senses. When we hit our finger with a hammer, stub our toes, or lean against a hot radiator, there is a fraction of a second delay before we realize the fact and yell, "Ouch!" This is the time it takes for the pain impulses to travel through our nervous system and register in our awareness. The same holds true for sound and sight. Visions and voices are recorded milliseconds after they actually occur, after they first impinge upon our eyes or our ears.

Our consciousness works a bit like a phenomenally quick Polaroid camera. An action is recorded, and a fraction of an instant later the print is developed and ready for viewing in our mind's eye.

Thus, you can never see or feel your own death. For the final snapshot is never developed for witnessing. As far as our ego is concerned, it will go on forever.

What a cruel joke we play on ourselves when our ego fears an event that it will never experience.

10.

There must be a division between our *ego* awareness, which ends with death, and our more *cosmic* awareness, which may well continue afterward.

It is cosmic awareness that manifests itself in sleep, in trance states, at the moment of orgasm, in religious ecstasy, during transcendent psychedelic journeys, and in pre-death experiences.

Thus it is that we can die and also live forever.

11.

While walking in the woods I came across a fallen tree that was decaying. It was impossible to say where the earth ended and where the tree began, as a fine powder seemed to emerge from the soil and enter the remaining trunk.

I'm sure that the earth doesn't remember that it once existed as a tree.

Nor does a phagocyte prowling through our blood vessels and tissues, alert and alive in its own right, have any knowledge that it exists within a body known as homo sapiens.

Are we, after all, so different from the phagocyte that we can conceive of the larger body that we reside in?

12.

The worm eats microbes, the fish swallows the worm, man eats the fish, and various microscopic creatures known as viruses and bacteria kill and digest man. Thus the cycle is perpetually repeated.

Death might be seen as nothing more than life feeding upon itself.

13.

When I go, I should like to be either thrown into the ocean and devoured by sharks, or planted in the fields of Bridgehampton, unpreserved, so that the grass and the weeds and the grubs might feed on me. I should like to go into other substances very quickly.

My "stuff" going into something else is a much cheerier idea than being dressed in a special suit, having makeup applied, and being embalmed so that I might lie there among the worms for three months before they dare to nibble at me.

14.

The French refer to the orgasm as "le petit mort," the little death. Sex has always born an intimate relationship with death.

Is the cry of the orgasm and the contortions on lovers faces so different from the sounds and strains of expiration?

Is the fusing, melting, ego transcendence that is felt during passionate lovemaking different from the experiences of falling mountain climbers, meditating monks, or psychedelic ecstasy?

Is it any accident that the grass grows greener beneath the hangman's noose because of the ejaculations that fell from so many of the men who hung there?

15.

Opposites define one another and create meaning.

"Up" is meaningless unless there is "down." "Day" makes no sense unless there is "night." "Tall" exists only if "short" does. Take away one of the polarities and the other disappears; it cannot stand alone. Amorphousness replaces the previous division.

So it is with life and death. You have to go off in order to go on, for you came out of nothing in the first place.

16.

At age seventy, a philosophical Albert Einstein wrote a letter to a rabbi, consoling him on the loss of his daughter, "a sinless, beautiful, sixteen-year-old child."

A human being is a part of the whole, called by us "Universe," a part limited in time and space. He experiences himself, his thoughts and feelings, as something separated from the rest—a kind of optical delusion of his consciousness. This delusion is a kind of prison for us, restricting us to our personal desires and to affection for a few persons nearest to us. Our task must be to free ourselves from this prison by widening our circle of compassion to embrace all living creatures and the whole nature in its beauty. Nobody is able to achieve this completely, but the striving for such achievement is in itself a part of the liberation and a foundation for inner security.

QUOTATIONS

The greatest danger, that of losing one's own self, may pass off quietly as if it were nothing; every other loss, that of an arm, a leg, five dollars, etcetera, is sure to be noticed.

—Sören Kierkegaard

The *concept* of death, with its prestructurings and imaginatings, has no actuality in life. The concept is the tragedy, not the event.

—Joseph Chilton Pearce

We sometimes congratulate ourselves at the moment of waking from a troubled dream: it may be so at the moment after death.

—Nathaniel Hawthorne

Man makes a death, which nature never made:
Then on the point of his own fancy falls;
And feels a thousand deaths, in fearing one.

—Edward Young

Death, so called, is a thing which makes men
   weep
And yet a third of life is passed in sleep.

—George Gordon, Lord Byron

No man can be ignorant that he must die, nor be sure that he may not this very day.

—Cicero

For life is nearer every day to death.

—Plato, *Phaedrus*

Death's but a path that must be trod
If man would ever pass to God.

—Parnell

How can death be evil when in its presence we are not aware of it?

—Diogenes

There is nothing dreadful in that which delivers from all that which is to be dreaded.

—Quintas Septimus Florens Tertullian

Thales said there was no difference between life and death. "Why then," said someone to him, "do not you die?" "Because," said he, "it makes no difference."

—Diogenes Laërtius

Life is the leading cause of death.

—overheard conversation

Death destroys a man; the idea of Death saves him.

—E. M. Forster

What is death? A bugbear

—Epictetus

Death is not the greatest of ills; it is worse to want to die and not be able to.

—Sophocles

A little sleep, a little slumber, a little folding of the hands to sleep.

—Proverbs 6: 10

It is good to die before one has done aɪything deserving death.

—Anaxandrides

He is miserable who dieth not before he desires to die.
—Thomas Fuller

Death may be the greatest of all human blessings.
—Socrates

Nothing can happen more beautiful than death.
—Walt Whitman

Death itself is nothing; but we fear
To be we know not what, we know not where.
—John Dryden

Done with the work of breathing; the mad race run through
to the end; the golden goal attained and found to be a hole.
—Ambrose Bierce

Man is the only animal that contemplates death, and also
the only animal that shows any sign of doubt of its finality.
—William Ernest Hocking

She died peacefully, in the certitude that death was not a
calamity.
—survivor of Belsen, describing the death of Anne Frank

To die will be an awfully big adventure.
—J. M. Barrie, *Peter Pan*

The living are the dead on holiday.
—Maurice Maeterlinck

There is no death. What seems so is transition. This life
of mortal breath is but a suburb of the life elysian, whose
portal we call death.
—Henry Wadsworth Longfellow

Judge none blessed before his death.

—Ecclesiastes 11: 28

Death is really nothing, for so long as we are, death has not come, and when it has come we are not.

—Epicurus

15

A Summing Up

"THE EARTH BELONGS to the living" was Jefferson's credo after the death of his wife and beloved children, and it is for the living that I've intended this book. By approaching the subject without panic, but also without trying to rob it of its inherent mystery, by discussing what is known and respecting what is unknown, I trust we may be able to have better deaths and endure more gracefully the deaths of those about us. Good deaths are not necessarily painless, nor are they pretty. They are human acts which do not trivialize life but heighten it. They dispel fear and have a dignity about them that gives meaning and importance both to survivors and the person dying.

Rather than death's signifying the zenith of one's life, our culture makes it the low point. Instead of providing the dying with intimacy and candor, it substitutes isolation and cant. A professional class of nurses, orderlies, doctors, clergymen, and undertakers have replaced family as our final caretakers. No wonder so many of us have trouble accepting death, when so few of us have closely witnessed its occurrence.

My view of death as an avoidable disaster led me to become a physician, my only partly disguised dread propelling me into a profession dedicated to overcoming this enemy. Surprisingly enough, being trained as a doctor did not initially lower my fearfulness as much as I might have anticipated. Yes, I did learn to medicate those on the way out and to examine dead bodies. But in my earlier years as a medical student and intern I wore a protective shield which prevented me from making intimate contact with the dying. I was busy playing the part of the optimistic physician, the cool professional who knew what he was doing. As such, I dared not hang about the seriously ill too long. If I did, I doubt whether I could have continued playing my game. Nor did I have enough ease with death to sit with those who were failing. These people brought me down emotionally, and like other medical personnel I avoided them as best I could.

This avoidance perpetuated both my ignorance and my deep apprehensions about dying. Yet my inability to overcome the Destroyer led eventually to a victory for life, to an appreciation of pulse, pattern, and cycle, of which existence and non-existence form an integral part. Sharing my father's death, spending more time with the dying, and constant contemplations of the entire process put me in touch with many affirmative aspects of death. These affirmations are verifiable by anyone willing to provide an atmosphere of caring concern for the dying; who are prepared to commit themselves to open and honest communication.

Familiarity with death, however, is not easy to come by, and the fact that so few Americans have such firsthand experiences makes it a self-perpetuating aversion. Professor Robert J. Kastenbaum, editor of *Omega: The Journal of Death and Dying,* and a psychologist at the University of Massachusetts, conducted an experiment in which housewives were asked to interview a falsified hospital patient. Some were told he was simply ill, others that he was dying of abdominal cancer. Those who thought he was sick responded warmly to him. The ones who believed he had a terminal disease seemed repelled, avoided eye contact, and distanced themselves.

Distancing ourselves from death not only insults and isolates the dying, but serves to reinforce our own fears, which have been programmed into us from birth. The beginnings of dread that register on a baby's face when mama, playing peek-a-boo, disappears behind the crib's headboard, and the squeals of delight when she reappears, are rivaled in intensity only by the exquisite tension and relief adults feel when undergoing or identifying with some life-and-death situation.

In India, as in certain other countries, the passage of life's time progresses from student to householder to the wisdom of age. By contrast, our model of the good life extends only through the late thirties. One receives a decent education in order to settle down, have children, and live in a comfortably furnished home. Lacking traditions, meaningful symbols, or roles for older people, too many of us wind up as discards, in homes for the aged, without respect and without a function. And we are missing a decent model for a good death. We have, certainly, honored deaths which occurred in battle, but we have failed to establish humane rituals or interactions for the type of death most of us will face.

I have tried to state both actions and principles that have proved useful to both the healthy and the ill as the final event unfolds: recognizing the confusion and the range of your emotional reactions, giving honest information and diagnosis to the dying person, evaluating alternatives to standard medical treatments, eliminating pain, ways of comforting those you care about, the advantages of dying at home, appreciating the problems that the family undergoes prior to and after the death of someone they love, making prudent financial arrangements, and methods of overcoming the fear of death. You have heard from those who are dying as well as from those who survived. I've presented accounts of after-death experiences and quotations by wise men and women throughout the ages that have added to my degree of comfort and tranquillity.

Ultimately, of course, every death is a unique phenomenon, one which each individual must resolve in his or her own particular way. These resolutions can be painful or affirmative, chaotic or centered, despairing or fulfilling. It is my belief that the traumas of dying can be largely alleviated through candid communication and a fuller understanding of the needs of both the surviving and the expiring.

Death is both a concept and a force that will touch each of our lives and the lives of all those we cherish. If this book helps generate a meaningful dialogue between the living and the dying, it will have fulfilled my purpose in writing it, for open communication—discussing our fears, our aversions, and our attitudes—remains our best hope for facing the truth of death with more directness and greater compassion.

Resources

1. COUNSELLING GROUPS

Make Today Count
218 South 6th Street
Burlington, Iowa 52601
phone (319) 754-8977

Forty branches throughout the United States and Canada. Founded by Orville Kelly, a middle-aged newspaper man with terminal cancer, this organization provides group sessions led by and for the dying, to help them with both the practical and emotional difficulties encountered during this period of life.

2. NURSING AND HOMEMAKING SERVICES

Visiting nurse and homemaker services may be located by consulting your local telephone directory ("Visiting nurse" and "Homemaker"), contacting your state social service department, or getting in touch with:

National League for Nursing
10 Columbus Circle
New York, N.Y. 10019
phone (212) 582-1022

3. ALTERNATIVES TO HOSPITAL CARE

Hospice, Inc.
765 Prospect Street
New Haven, Conn. 06511
phone (203) 787-5871

This facility is in touch with other such organizations starting elsewhere in the country and can provide contacts to help in arranging for home care of the terminally ill and for institutions that are more flexible and humanistic than the typical hospital.

4. SPECIAL CARE FOR SPECIAL ILLNESSES

American Cancer Society
219 East 42 Street
New York, N.Y. 10017
phone (212) 867-3700

Provides information on the disease process and will supply the address of your local chapter, which might help arrange for homemaking and home-nursing services.

American Heart Association
44 East 23 Street
New York, N.Y. 10010
phone (212) 533-1100

Similar services and information for heart patients.

Other, more unusual illnesses, often have their own foundations. Your local medical association or hospital ought to be able to provide names and addresses. Some of these foundations will also supply special care and facilities.

5. FUNERAL ARRANGEMENTS

Continental Association of Funeral and Memorial Societies
1828 L Street
Washington, D.C. 20036
(202) 293-4821

Local memorial societies can be looked up in your phone directory or yellow pages. If you cannot locate one in your area, ask for help from your local funeral director, or contact the above-listed Washington, D.C., office.

6. SUPPLEMENTARY PAYMENTS AND BENEFITS

Information on benefits is available from your local Social Security office (listed in your telephone directory under "U.S. Government").

Other benefits are available through the Veterans' Administration ("U.S. Government").

Emergency funds and facilities may also be inquired about from your state or municipal department of social services.

Selected Readings

Alsop, Stewart. *Stay of Execution: A Sort of Memoir.* Philadelphia: Lippincott, 1973.

Alvarez, A. *The Savage God, a Study of Suicide.* New York: Random House, 1972.

Caine, Lynn. *Widow.* New York: Morrow, 1974.

Faulkner, William. *As I Lay Dying.* New York: Random House, 1930.

Kübler-Ross, Elisabeth. *On Death and Dying.* New York: Macmillan, 1970.

218SOMEONE YOU LOVE IS DYING

Leary, Timothy; Metzner, Ralph; and Alpert, Richard. *The Psychedelic Experience. A Manual Based On The Tibetian Book Of The Dead.* New Hyde Park, New York:University Press, 1964.

Lifton, Robert Jay, and Olson, Eric. *Living and Dying.* New York: Praeger, 1974.

Mannes, Marya. *Last Rights, a Case for the Good Death.* New York: Morrow, 1973.

Mitford, Jessica. *The American Way of Death.* New York: Simon and Schuster, 1963.

Pearson, Leonard, ed. *Death and Dying, Current Issues in the Treatment of the Dying Person.* Cleveland: Case Western Reserve University Press, 1969.

Ram Dass. *Be Here Now.* San Cristobal, New Mexico: Lama Foundation, 1971.

Watts, Alan. *The Book: On the Taboo Against Knowing Who You Are.* New York: Pantheon, 1966.

————. *Cloud Hidden-Whereabouts Unknown.* New York: Pantheon, 1973.

Yutang, Lin. *The Wisdom of Lao Tse.* New York: Random House, 1948.

Suggested Films

Cries and Whispers. Director, Ingmar Bergman, 1972.
El Topo. Director, Alejandro Jodorowski, 1970.
The Holy Mountain. Director, Alejandro Jodorowski, 1973.
Hospital. Director, Arthur Miller, 1972.
Ikiru. Director, Akira Kurosawa, 1952.
The Loved One. Director, Tony Richardson, 1965.
Odd Man Out. Director, Carol Reed, 1947.
The Shop on Main Street. Directors, Jan Kadar and Elmar Klos, 1965.

Death rides on every passing breeze,
He lurks in every flower.
—Bishop Heber

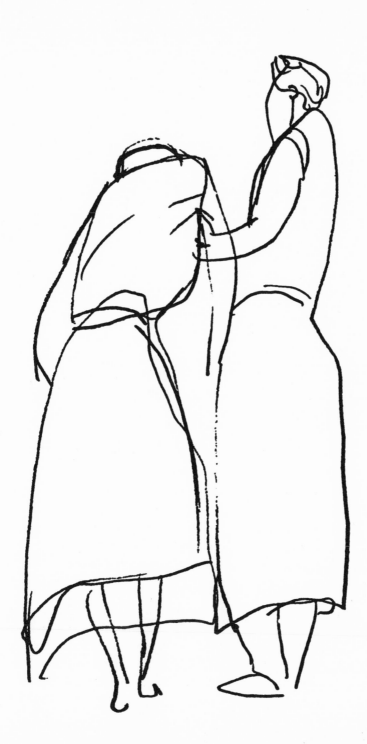